REALSIMPLE

THE ORGANIZED HOME

REAL SIMPLE

THE ORGANIZED HOME

from the editors of *Real Simple*

Written by Kendell Cronstrom

Produced by Melcher Media, Inc. for Real Simple and Time Inc. Home Entertainment

contents

Even before *Real Simple* launched in the spring of 2000, it was clear that this enterprise was so much more than a magazine. The notion that there were CLEAR, BEAUTIFUL, COMPLETELY USEFUL WAYS TO MAKE LIFE EASIER AND BETTER was a powerful one—so much so that it was destined to grow beyond the pages that so many dedicated readers buy on the newsstand or find in their mailboxes.

And so…the book you now hold in your hands. *Real Simple: The Organized Home* is inspired by *Real Simple* magazine's best advice on organizing your living space—a clutter-busting, timesaving, space-maximizing road map, so to speak. Of course, ORGANIZATION MEANS DIFFERENT THINGS AT DIFFERENT TIMES AND IN DIFFERENT SPACES. Sometimes it means paring down (donating half your attic to charity). Sometimes it means adding (finding the perfect shower caddy). But the goal is always the same: to make order out of chaos, to bring a sense of control, meaning, and ease to your rich, complicated, busy life.

This book can help you do just that.

For many people, the idea of getting organized is far more daunting than the reality of doing it. If you need an incentive to start, keep in mind that A SMALL INVESTMENT OF TIME NOW WILL HAVE A LARGE PAYOFF LATER.

American women spend 55.2 minutes a day looking for things, according to a study *Real Simple* conducted in 2003. Those 55.2 minutes per day add up to a staggering 14 days per year. Just IMAGINE THE FREE TIME (the two-week vacation!) you'd have if you always knew exactly where to find your car keys/scarf/favorite recipe/new earrings. You'll have it once you use this book.

Remember—you don't need to tackle all your rooms at once. Approach this book as you would approach your own house: Enter the foyer and proceed into the living and family rooms to the kitchen, the bedroom, the bathroom, and beyond. In each chapter you'll find the basic necessities for EASY, STYLISH, ORGANIZED LIVING—think of them as the building blocks of every room—and techniques to make everything in a given room work together. Whether you're organizing utensils, arranging books on shelves, or trying to decide how tall your new coffee table needs to be, the pages of *Real Simple: The Organized Home* have the answer. Follow the principles described in these pages, apply them to your own life, and just watch as those 55.2 minutes a day become a lot more fun.

Kristin van Ogtrop

the foyer

A foyer might seem like little more than a hallway with a front door attached, but in some ways it's the most important space in your home. It sets a mood, establishes your personality, and sends a message to your guests. In other words, it should be as inviting as possible. But that doesn't mean you have to spend a fortune on it. A single flower, a convenient bench, or a softly scented candle will let visitors and family alike know how much you care about your house—and them.

DOORMATS

Before anyone sets foot in the house, establish a tone just outside the front door. Besides being a hint of what's to come, doormats provide your first line of defense against household dirt. Also consider placing a washable cotton rug inside the front door. Outdoors or indoors, shoe-wiping should be enthusiastically encouraged.

BENCH

Even a narrow foyer can usually accommodate a long bench, which is both practical and pleasing to the eye. People can sit down on it while they remove their shoes or place parcels on it as they take off their coats. Rustic wooden benches and country-style painted versions have always been popular, but don't overlook benches with built-in storage (some have compartments or shelves beneath the seat; others have a hidden area beneath a flip-top seat). For benches that aren't padded, add a soft seat cushion in a soothing fabric that complements your entryway's decor.

MIRROR

Even the least self-conscious among us are grateful for a mirror near the front door. A foyer mirror gives guests a chance to freshen their appearance before proceeding farther into your house, and it lets you do a final check before going out or greeting company. A mirror also helps make the space seem larger and reflects light from windows, which can be especially advantageous in a dark entry hall.

BASKET

A tall basket—in a material ranging from natural woven rush to perforated stainless steel, depending on your taste—is a convenient catchall for umbrellas, hats, mittens, and other last-minute accessories. If you prefer that people not wear shoes in your home, a low, shallow basket makes a good container for house slippers or short-term shoe storage. Baskets should be attractive enough to be placed prominently next to (or tucked underneath) a hall table or just inside the front door.

LIGHTING

Nobody likes a dark house, and a dark foyer is especially uninviting. No matter which light fixture you choose—a sparkling chandelier says one thing, an elegant pendant lamp another—it should match the decor and provide enough light. Don't limit your options to overhead lighting: Sconces on either side of a mirror or a lamp on a hall table will add instant warmth and character.

five easy pieces

organization

Every inch counts in a foyer, where people come and go—and where shoes, coats, and gloves come off and go on.

bench

UTILIZE Family members and guests should sit on the bench, remove their shoes and hats, and then place them on a shelf or in a bin, keeping the main hallway from looking like a yard sale.

wall-mounted storage

SELECT Hooks, pegs, shelving units, or ledges, mounted on a wall within easy reach (six feet from the floor works well in most foyers), can be a lifesaver for homeowners who are short on entry-hall space. They come in many shapes, sizes, and finishes.

MOUNT It's wise not to mount pegs and hooks so close to the wall that whatever hangs from them scratches or smudges it—a little breathing room helps. Never mount pegs or hooks on a front door: Sweaters or coats look sloppy hanging from them, and an accidentally slammed door will very likely deposit everything on the floor.

small things

ARRANGE Shoes not stored on bench shelving can be lined up on a shoe rack (usually two shelves tall) or a shoe mat (placed on the floor). These often feature an open-slatted surface that allows wet shoes to dry.

HANG Try to get kids in the habit of hanging their backpacks on pegs or stowing them under the bench when they get home from school, or taking them directly to their bedrooms instead.

the hall closet Your last

stop out the door or first on your way in, the hall closet is

equal parts room-saver and rummage sale: It's the first

place to deposit anything you want out of sight—

jackets, tennis shoes, tote bags, umbrellas, and unmatched

soccer cleats—and the first place to get messy and

disorganized. (Understandably, too. When you get home,

you want to relax, not color-code and size-order the

family's windbreakers.) The chaos of coats, scarves, and

swim goggles can be easily tamed with a system that's

easy to keep in place—just like everything in the closet.

what belongs where

If you are fortunate enough to have a closet in your foyer, do not use it as a dumping ground for unfinished rolls of wrapping paper, the vacuum cleaner, and vintage Darth Vader masks.

STORE Hats, gloves, scarves, and other accessories belong in this space, in roll-out bins or boxes arranged on shelves, or even on the floor.

ARRANGE Shoes and boots can be lined up on the floor or even hung from the clothing rod in a shoe organizer.

coats

It's important to decide which coats and related outerwear accessories need to be kept in the foyer closet year-round. Winter parkas, dressy evening coats, and spring windbreakers can be stored in other closets in the house and moved to the foyer closet during the appropriate season, leaving space free for guests' things.

the measurements

A standard closet measures four feet across, which leaves room for about ten to thirteen coats. But you'll need room for guests' coats, too.

MODIFY If you have an extra-deep closet, such as one tucked under a stairway, consider installing a clothing rod in the back of the space so that you can rotate coats and jackets by season, or leave space on the front rod for visitors' coats.

AUGMENT Throwing a party? Even if you have a generously sized hall closet, you probably don't have room for the coats of fifty cocktail-party guests. Consider buying an inexpensive rolling garment rack and place it against the foyer wall that sees the least action.

PAINTED RUNNER

If you have wood floors that aren't
in particularly good shape, an inexpensive fix is to paint a runner with
two coats of acrylic latex sealed with
polyurethane.

COATRACK

Don't despair if the closet nearest
your foyer is upstairs and at the end of
the hall. There's a good reason the
coatrack has been around for at least
a century. The best versions have hooks
and pegs for hats, gloves, and coats,
as well as small shelves for keys and
wallets and attachments for shoes.

KEY AND MAIL TRAY

Avoid running back inside at the last
minute to find your keys or grab
your glasses. Keep a tray by the door
to hold the things you always mean
to take with you but too often forget.

CORNER SHOE MAT

If you have a low-traffic corner in your
entryway, invest in a wedge-shaped
shoe mat with slightly raised ridges,
which allow wet umbrellas and boots
to dry thoroughly.

INDIVIDUAL IN-BOX

Instead of one jumbled disarray
of catalogs, letters, permission slips,
and invitations, sort everything
into hanging bins assigned to each
family member.

ALL-PURPOSE ORGANIZER

A compartmentalized canvas organizer
is handy for sunglasses, keys, house
slippers, and the like. Buy one that
folds up neatly, so that you can stow it
when not in use.

the living room

The living room is no longer the last bastion of all things breakable. Towering curio cabinets have been replaced by more sensible side tables and consoles; coffee tables can handle a lot more than a dainty after-dinner demitasse; expensive upholstery has surrendered to more comfortable, cleanable slipcovers. And the sofa is now something people can actually sink into, rather than perch on the edge of. While it is still the most formal space in the house, the living room has lightened up a bit, accommodating the ever-changing needs of the twenty-first-century family. With a little practical advice about the basic pieces and what goes where, you, your loved ones, and your guests can simply sit back and relax.

SOFA

Never skimp on a sofa—an inexpensive, poorly made one will soon show its weak spots. A well-constructed sofa should have eight-way hand-tied springs and a framework of kiln-dried wood, preferably a hardwood such as maple, which will not warp. You can save some money with the cushions: Fillings vary (down, feathers, cotton or synthetic batting, and foam, alone or in combination), with the general rule that you pay more cash for more cushion. Delicate fabrics such as silk do not wear well and fade under harsh sunlight (linen can fade, too, but it is fairly hardy); washable slipcovers or a sturdier upholstery fabric will better protect your investment.

OCCASIONAL CHAIR

The same principles for choosing a sofa apply to an occasional chair, which is ideal for a living room because it both looks great arranged with other furniture and can stand alone in a corner for reading. The most practical, modern examples have generously padded arms, seats, and backs; by contrast, wing chairs tend to look stiffer and feel less comfortable and inviting.

COFFEE TABLE

It's also known as a cocktail table, although nowadays it's more likely to display books and flowers. Most decorating professionals agree that a coffee table should stand about seventeen inches tall—the average seat height for sofas and chairs—putting everything within reach. Materials make a marked difference: It is much easier to clean a spill or smudge on glass, but glass is also potentially dangerous for small children. Wood can look very beautiful but is prone to nicks and water rings; metal tables can withstand a lot of abuse but are often heavy and sharp-edged.

SIDE TABLE

Sometimes the most important role is that of a supporting player. Not everyone at your gatherings will be within arm's reach of the coffee table, so you may need an accessory table (or two). Side tables should be both large and stable enough to hold drinks, plates of food, books, lamps, and decorative accessories. Many also have drawers and lower shelves for more storage or display space.

LAMPS

Lamps challenge even the most seasoned decorators. It's difficult to find a pair of antique lamps in good condition (with shades that haven't been battered from frequent use). And contemporary lamps can be prohibitively expensive (except for some versions found at stores such as Target, Restoration Hardware, and Crate & Barrel). To take lamps you already own from humdrum to high class, focus your energies on their shades. A few rules of thumb: A shade should be about three-quarters the height of the lamp base and roughly mirror the shape of the lamp. If your lamp isn't too heavy, take it with you to the shade store to ensure a perfect match. Colored shades and shades trimmed with inexpensive ribbon or other edging provide extra pizzazz.

five easy pieces

basics

helpful additions

MIRROR

A mirror hung above a mantel or behind a sofa gives the living room the illusion of space. It also enhances the room's ambience by reflecting light from lamps, candles, and windows. Choose large, seemingly over-scale mirrors that will fill up a wall; a puny mirror will look cutesy and insubstantial.

OTTOMAN

The chameleon of the living room, an ottoman provides extra seating at parties and a place to rest tired feet at the end of a long day. With a tray on its surface, it becomes an ersatz coffee table on which you can display art books and rest a drink. Some ottomans contain storage com-partments beneath a lidded top, providing a space for stowing magazines or CDs.

ÉTAGÈRE

A no-nonsense shelving unit with a fancy name, an étagère is indispensable in living rooms filled with mementos and decorative accessories that otherwise have no place to go. A living room with knick-knacks arranged on every available surface looks cluttered, but an étagère will keep it all in order. Placed behind a sofa or between two seating areas, an étagère can also act as a room divider. Shop for one that offers both strength and character, such as brass with glass shelves or bamboo.

SCREEN

At first glance, a screen might seem like excessive orna-mentation, but it can work wonders in a living area, acting as a room divider and also cordoning off anything you might not want guests to see, such as an electronics cabinet in the corner or an air-conditioning vent.

CONVERSATION PIECES

Gewgaws, bibelots, mementos, tchotchkes, dust collectors: Call them what you will, but definitely give some thought to how you display them. To make an impact, small collections of objects—cobalt-glass vases, Italian ceram-ics, African masks—should be displayed in groups, not arrayed here and there throughout the room.

floors, walls, windows, lighting

CARPETS

Most carpets produced today are made of tufted synthetic fibers, although woven wool and wool-blend varieties are still a popular (but more expensive) choice. Synthetic fibers are not particularly absorbent and therefore don't stain easily, but they also don't dye as nicely or feel as plush as wool. Consider the room when you consider the rug. If your living room is a high-traffic area, you'll benefit from a synthetic carpet with a tight pile: It's less likely to fray and will last longer. But if your living room is mostly off-limits (or off-limits to shoes, anyway), you can indulge in a more luxurious wool version with a looser pile.

BARE WOOD OR AREA RUGS

A bare wood floor can be beautiful, but it is susceptible to scuff marks and scratches and should be regularly swept and mopped to maintain its luster. It also does not absorb noise well and is obviously chillier underfoot than a carpet. An area rug will show off the wood while protecting it and providing contrast; it also acts as a sound buffer and adds warmth. A loosely tufted area rug is not advisable, since the edge will most likely trip people up and wear quickly; you're better off with a tightly piled synthetic rug or a natural material such as sea grass edged in a heavy-duty linen.

PAINT OR WALLPAPER

Paint is the greatest decorating tool of all time: For shockingly little money, you can utterly transform a space, whether it's a small apartment or a palatial house. And thanks to advances in paint technology, most finishes, such as semigloss and gloss enamels, can be washed clean with little effort. (The exception, however, is flat latex paint; it tends to wear and streak when washed, although advances in its care are being made.) Check with your paint supplier to be sure which paint will work best for you. Or consider wallpaper. Newer versions are easier to hang than their delicate forebears and can be cleaned with ease.

CURTAINS OR SHADES

Curtains and shades add ornamentation and privacy to a room while diffusing and blocking light. Curtains are generally more decorative but also more fragile: Whether grandly gathered and swagged or allowed to fall simply to the floor, they require careful cleaning and regular maintenance. Curtains made of delicate fabrics can also fade under harsh sunlight. Shades, on the other hand, usually fit neatly within a window frame or just outside it and roll up smoothly in decorative folds or pleats. While they are easier to care for than curtains, they lack character and are best put to use in children's or family rooms. A nice compromise for a living room is an attractive curtain with a discreet shade behind it.

LIGHTING

Overhead lighting in a living room is often harsh on the eyes and less than flattering to even the most wrinkle-free face, unless you use reduced-wattage bulbs that cast a soft (rather than bright white) light. In most instances, a better option is a variety of table and floor lamps, which project diffuse rather than direct light and flatter both furnishings and faces. (Your guests will thank you.)

organization

furniture

How do you create a living room that is both a serene oasis and a practical gathering spot? Easy—by scrutinizing the space, assessing your needs, and editing.

arranging the furniture

GROUP No guest at a party (and certainly no member of the family) should feel as if she can't hear what's going on, so make sure that your furniture is grouped so people can talk.

GATHER A small living room requires just one gathering of furniture, but larger rooms can handle two or more.

FOCUS Seating should be arrayed around a focal point, such as a fireplace or window. Rarely can you place sofas or chairs alone against a wall without making guests feel as if they're trapped in a police lineup.

COMFORT Make sure that every spot, be it a chair or a sofa cushion, is within range of a coffee or side table. You and your guests need somewhere to put down your drinks.

ensuring easy access

DISPLAY It's wonderful to have all of your heirloom furniture on display, but only if you don't trip over it on your way to the powder room or kitchen.

FLOW Each seating area should have at least two ways in or out, and, except for side tables, most pieces of furniture should be at least eighteen inches apart so people can pass easily between them.

choosing pieces that work for you

MOVE If you entertain often, consider investing in pieces that have casters: They can be moved easily to accommodate different groups of people.

HIDE Storage ottomans are ideal for quickly stowing items—such as a stack of magazines, a stash of Playmobil people, or a delicate woven cashmere throw that might not be up to the extra traffic—and holding trays of food and drinks in lieu of a coffee table.

PROTECT Splurge on a slipcover for your valuable sofa or club chair if you like to entertain without having to worry about damage and spills.

organization

The people who hang on your walls and the artwork that fills your rooms deserve special treatment.

photographs and artwork

the right frame

SELECT Your choice of frame is as personal as your choice of artwork. Photographs are best mounted on acid- and lignin-free mats, which keep them from sticking to the glass and ultimately deteriorating. Photos dry-mounted by a professional framer survive humidity best.

the right arrangement

SINGLE PIECES Large pieces of art function best alone. Smaller pieces are more powerful when arranged in groups and/or by theme. A large print should be big enough to hold its own above a sofa or mantel, but not so big as to overpower it.

GROUPS Photographs framed and matted in complementary materials and hung in tight clusters (no more than two inches apart) become works of art in their own right. You can also hang them in geometrical configurations—horizontal or vertical lines, grids, squares—without fear.

the right place

EVALUATE Always measure carefully, marking lightly on the wall with pencil, and taking into consideration not just the width and height of the frame but also the space you want around its perimeter. Never hang artwork less than eighteen inches from the top of a sofa or chair, since someone's head could hit it.

organization

books

In addition to enriching the mind, books can enrich a living room's decor.

in bookcases

ARRANGE Most fiction, reference works, and standard-size books can be placed in bookcases in the living room—particularly in ones affixed to a wall. (Freestanding versions are not advisable unless they are extremely sturdy and anchored to a wall or the floor.)

MIX IT UP If the arrangement of titles on shelves is too monotonous, try interspersing groups of books with ceramics or other objects. You can also alternate clustering groups of books vertically and horizontally for visual interest.

on the shelf

CATEGORIZE A smart way to organize your books is to group them by size first and subject matter (or author) second. Hardcover books, with or without their dust jackets, are generally more appealing in the living room than dog-eared paperbacks.

around the room

PILE IT UP Oversize art or "coffee-table" books can be attractively stacked flat in piles on coffee and side tables as well as on ottomans, with spines facing outward to promote comment and conversation. Also consider placing a small stack on a fireplace mantel or little-used side table or bench.

THE WORK OF CHARLES AND RAY EAMES   ABRAMS | LIBRARY OF CONGRESS | VITRA DESIGN MUSEUM

SZARKOWSKI   ALFRED STIEGLITZ AT LAKE GEORGE   THE MUSEUM OF MODERN ART, NEW YORK

Seuil   Henri Cartier-Bresson / Paris à vue d'œil

Rembrandt's Landscapes: Drawing and Prints

HARRY CALLAHAN   NATIONAL GALLERY OF ART · BULFINCH

JOHN
RKOWSKI   A T G E T   The Museum of
Modern Art | Callaway

THE HISTORY OF DECORATIVE ARTS
THE RENAISSANCE AND MANNERISM IN EUROPE

TALL BASEBOARDS

Replace standard three-inch baseboards with taller ones—they will make the room look loftier.

MIRRORS

A mirror always amplifies a space. Make sure it reflects something you don't mind seeing twice, such as a lovely bookcase, mantel, or view of the outdoors.

SLIPCOVERS

A relatively affordable way to change the look of your living room without adding another piece of furniture is to slipcover what you have. That way, you can even create two or more looks for different times of the year.

CURTAINED WINDOWS

Curtains don't necessarily need to hang from (or within) the window frame. A small window can look much larger if you install curtains on the wall above it, making sure that the fabric drapes over the frame and hides it.

STRIPED WALLS

Just as a vertically striped shirt makes a person look taller and thinner, so can a striped wallpaper (or simply painted stripes) work magic in a low-ceilinged room.

BOLD COLORS

White is refreshing and airy in a room, but it isn't always the best color choice. A common decorating myth holds that dark colors make rooms look smaller, but they can actually make a room and its furnishings appear bolder and larger.

the family room

THE FAMILY ROOM   In some homes the living room doubles as the family room, and in others the family room is a separate space entirely (and may go by a different name, too: den, TV room, library, playroom, sunroom). But no matter what you call it or how you use it, organizing the room will help you enjoy it. While it's always important to make good use of shelves, drawers, and other storage areas, the family room shouldn't be so tidy that everyone is discouraged from crossing the threshold. Convenient access to reading materials, electronics, and games is key to getting the most out of the space, so make sure the room is set up with the whole family in mind.

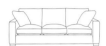

SOFA

A family-room sofa can be a little slouch-ier, and a little softer, than a more formal living-room sofa. Upholstered in an inexpensive cotton, it can take a beating and be recovered with-out breaking the bank. Piled high with pillows, it becomes the ultimate comfort zone for watching television or settling in with a good book.

COFFEE TABLE

If you like to have a coffee table in the family room—for bowls of popcorn or a cup of tea—make sure it has a drawer in it (or a tray on top of it) to hold the various remote controls you need to keep up with the electronic age. A family-room coffee table can also be a little lower than the standard seventeen-inch-high living-room one: Items on a shorter table are less likely to block your view.

RECLINER

No longer an impos-sible-to-move, vinyl-clad giant, the recliner has been stream-lined and souped up, calibrated to recline in more positions, and covered in comfortable fabrics that work with your decor. And most recliners can now fit demurely in a corner without taking up as much valuable space as before—even when fully extended.

SIDE TABLE

With or without drawers, side tables can be catchalls for the accoutrements of family living, from remotes to reading glasses. In a room with heavy foot traffic, you'll want side tables with sturdy bases, so that rambunctious children (or clumsy adults) don't send them flying.

LAMPS

Table lamps are useful for reading, but you might also consider floor lamps, which can be placed in low-traffic corners and cast light at an angle into the room. While overhead lighting is generally not desirable in a living room because of the unflattering shad-ows it casts, in the family room it can illuminate activities such as reading the newspaper and playing board games.

five easy pieces

basics

helpful additions

MEDIA CABINET

Any family room will benefit from a media cabinet. Instead of stacking the stereo receiver, DVD player, and TV set in a precarious pile, you can arrange them in an orderly, logical fashion on the shelves of a media cabinet, which may also have drawers or cubbyholes for organizing your CD, DVD, and video-cassette collections. Choose a solid wood cabinet that can withstand the weight of your electronic equipment; avoid those with insubstantial veneers, which often flake away with regular use.

CONSOLE TABLE

A console is a tall, long, narrow table usually placed behind a sofa or against a wall. It makes a wonderful surface for displaying framed photos and other accessories and also helps define areas: Behind a sofa, it can separate one section of the room from another, creating distinct spaces for children and adults, for example.

OTTOMAN

Some ottomans have lids and storage compartments, which come in handy for hiding away games and magazines. They also provide extra seating for guests and for watching TV.

PILLOWS

If you don't have the time or money to slipcover your sofa or favorite reading chair—much less buy a new one—try tossing a few pillows in contrasting colors and patterns on the cushions. You can find an extraordinary variety of affordable pillows at home furnishings boutiques and chain stores such as Pottery Barn and Crate & Barrel. Foam and other hypo-allergenic stuffers are best for family members who are sensitive to feathers and down.

THROWS

The same pillow principles apply to throws, which can add instant panache to a drab sofa or chair (and are great at camouflaging your failed efforts to remove a stain). A throw in a weight and fabric similar to those of the upholstery will seem like another layer of luxury. (For example, a cashmere throw would work on a thick wool-covered sofa.) You can change a sofa or chair's character—formal to informal, summer to fall—by simply rotating throws. You can also change your own character— from freezing to toasty—by wrapping yourself in a throw and bypassing a trip to the thermostat. Because they are exposed to dust and vulnerable to staining, throws must be cleaned regularly.

organization

You can't find that Norah Jones CD you're looking for—and you know it's in this room *somewhere*. But with these simple strategies, you can always put your hands on your music and movies, your tapes and discs.

drawers

ORGANIZE If you choose to keep CDs, DVDs, videocassettes, and audiocassettes in their original plastic cases, they can often be placed alphabetically (or by theme) in a desk drawer.

shelves

ASSIGN Shelving is also an excellent organizational tool. One or two subject categories—such as rock/pop, jazz—can be placed on each shelf. The discs or cassettes should then be arranged alphabetically.

notebooks

CATEGORIZE The plastic cases for CDs and DVDs can take up a lot of space and tend to fall apart. But you can remove the cases and use books with special plastic-sleeve inserts, which are ideal for organizing and protecting the discs from dust. Organize discs by category in alphabetical order, and be sure to label the spine of each book so that you can pull the right one from the shelf.

organization

photographs

Photographs can be invaluable records of a dream vacation or an important family gathering, but too many of them can be overwhelming.

boxes and albums

SELECT Start by editing your photos, keeping only the shots that are unrepetitive and in focus. (You can always hold on to the negatives in case you change your mind about the images you've discarded.)

CLASSIFY Place the prints and negatives inside their original envelopes, label and date them by trip or event, and file them in acid-free storage boxes, which will help keep the prints from yellowing.

STORE Most storage boxes are attractive enough to keep on shelves; be sure not to put them in rooms subject to high heat, humidity, or dampness, such as an attic, a garage, or a basement.

HIGHLIGHT For reminiscing and entertaining guests, choose the best photos from a trip or family occasion and place them in a mini-album that's about the same size as the photographs themselves. Keep the albums in a drawer or on a shelf.

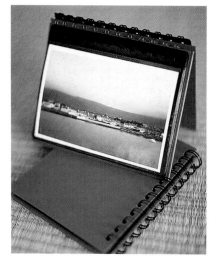

casual display

CREATE Not every photograph on a wall has to be framed beautifully (and expensively); sometimes a humbler treatment works better. Make use of dime-store and flea-market frames, or skip frames entirely and hang photographs in simple mats (just be sure the mats are made of acid-free material). Change your displays periodically by slipping in new pictures.

toys and games

A gargantuan wooden toy chest just doesn't work, especially when you're trying to find Barbie in a sea of stuffed animals and doll furniture.

getting started

SEPARATE To make child's play out of organizing your kids' stuff, start by dumping all the toys on the floor. Group them by set and then by size: small, medium, and large.

STORE Decide on the proper containers for each category. Ask your children to help you do this: They will learn basic organizing skills and also be more likely to remember which pieces go where.

containers

ASSESS Invest in see-through plastic storage containers in various sizes, and repurpose other storage devices such as shoe organizers, canvas totes, and plastic shoe boxes. To allow your child to play with toys in more than one room, buy a container on wheels.

location

STORE Place large containers on the floor or on the bottom of a bookshelf. (If you are short on space or have no shelving, consider storing toys in stacking units on the floor—but not so high that they'll endanger your child.) Art supplies and other messy items can go on a high shelf that only you can reach.

SUBSTITUTE SHELVING

A pricey wooden shelving system or cabinet is likely to see lots of wear and tear, so consider an inexpensive, sturdy chrome unit instead. If you like, top it off with a fabric cover.

INSTANT COVER-UP

Stains on your white cotton sofa? Cover them up—and add personality to the family room—with an attractive blanket or throw.

STREAMLINER

Corral all your loose electronic cords by sheathing them in plastic tubing, and label each cord for easy identification.

CLEAN CORNER

Stow materials for on-the-spot emergency cleanups on one discreet shelf in the family room.

LAMPSHADE UPGRADE

Rather than buy an expensive new shade, consider a trim. Apply a thin layer of Elmer's or fabric glue to the top and bottom edges of your shade, then apply pieces of ribbon, carefully joining the diagonally cut ends.

LARGE AREA RUGS

On wood floors, use a large area rug rather than a dinky one. It will make your furniture—and the room itself—seem much more pulled together.

the kitchen

An organized kitchen is a home's heart and soul, its central command station in a complicated age. While you can stuff it to the gills with gleaming accessories and appliances, no device will make your life easier if you don't know how to put it to work for you—and too many will actually thwart your efforts to make the room run smoothly. To create a serene, efficient kitchen, instill a sense of order. Think about which tools serve you best, then create an organizational system based on the items you use most and those you use only occasionally. Apply this method at all levels, from paring knives and vegetable peelers to drawers and shelving units to storage for pots and pans and cleaning supplies. You'll spend less time laboring over the stove and more time savoring its rewards.

WHISK essential tools

WOODEN SPOONS

Metal spoons can scratch pans; plastic spoons are prone to scorching and melting. As long as they are not used near an open flame, wooden spoons are your best bet in the kitchen. Affordable and lightweight, they are gentle on both food and the pot it's cooked in.

STAINLESS-STEEL MIXING BOWLS

Anyone who likes to cook needs more than one bowl: for separating liquid ingredients from dry, for preparing salad dressing and greens before tossing them together. Stainless-steel bowls are lightweight and clean easily, whereas plastic bowls can't handle hot ingredients, and glass bowls can be too heavy.

RUBBER SPATULAS

Although a rubber spatula will melt over a hot stove, nothing beats it for getting batter out of a bowl, molasses and corn syrup out of a measuring cup, and peanut butter out of the jar. You can also use it to frost a cake.

MEASURING CUPS

Careful measuring is one key to a positive outcome in the kitchen. Measuring cups come in many different sizes and often in sets: A two-cup measuring cup will meet most of your needs, though many cooks like the eight-cup Pyrex version because it doubles as a mixing bowl.

WHISK

A wire whisk beats, blends, and mixes as much or as little as you want—no electric mixer can be that precise. Ideal for scrambling eggs or whipping cream, it's also handy as a substitute sifter—put dry ingredients into a bowl and whisk them together.

COLANDER

A stainless-steel colander drains freshly washed fruits and vegetables and just-cooked pasta. Choose one with a sturdy pedestal base (individual feet can get rickety over time and bend or break off). Don't buy a flimsy plastic colander; it stains easily and can warp when exposed to hot water.

VEGETABLE PEELER

Both the old-time slim model and the Y-shaped variant streamline kitchen prep. In addition to peeling fruit and vegetables, you can also use a peeler to make chocolate shavings for desserts and slice thin curls of Parmesan or other hard cheeses.

TONGS

Tongs are an extension of your hand. They're indispensable for flipping meats over a high flame and just as suitable for plucking a bay leaf out of soup, stir-frying vegetables, transferring ingredients from counter or bowl to pan, or turning potatoes as they bake.

RASP

This skinny, flat tool (also called a zester, or grater, or microplane) was designed for zesting citrus fruits, but it's also wonderful for shredding carrots and finely grating hard cheese. It's easy to position directly over a mixing bowl or pot.

KITCHEN SHEARS

Kitchen shears, preferably made of heavy-gauge stainless steel with easy-to-grip plastic handles, cut down on time spent in the kitchen. You can snip fresh herbs with them, cut a whole chicken into pieces, or open tightly wrapped packages.

pots and pans

EIGHT-QUART STOCKPOT

A pot made of anodized aluminum is more affordable and easier to lift than its heavy metal counterparts. The best products on the market come with a pasta insert, which lets you drain your pasta without dragging the entire pot to the sink; even better are those that also include a steamer insert for vegetables.

THREE-QUART SAUTÉ PAN

This versatile workhorse can cook everything from scrambled eggs to a T-bone steak. Choose a stainless-steel version with an inner core of aluminum or copper, both of which conduct heat better than plain stainless steel. Lids should be snug and topped with an easy-to-grasp, heatproof knob or handle.

TWO-QUART SAUCEPAN

Whether you want to reheat soup or make a meat sauce, a copper pan is your best option, since copper responds well to precise temperature settings. A combined-metal version (stainless steel with a copper or aluminum core) is the next best thing, and is also a lot less expensive.

small appliances

MICROWAVE OVEN

The 1970s behemoth is now slimmer and less expensive (there are even microwave/toaster-oven combinations). The only machine on the planet that can both defrost a chicken and pop popcorn is also a handy sous-chef, boiling water, melting butter, and softening brown sugar in a flash.

TOASTER OVEN

About nine out of ten American households have a toaster, yet a toaster oven can do so much more. Besides browning your morning waffle, a toaster oven can roast vegetables, broil lean meats or fish, bake cookies, reheat leftovers, and warm up store-bought foods.

FOOD PROCESSOR

The appliance that revolutionized baking (making homemade bread a pleasure rather than a chore) also does nearly all the prep work for multi-ingredient recipes—chopping, slicing, and dicing instantly.

HANDHELD BLENDER

This smart tool can do much of the work of a handheld mixer and an upright blender, pureeing a soup directly in the stockpot (avoiding pot-to-blender spills) and whipping cream in seconds. It is also ergonomically correct, giving you complete control.

COFFEE GRINDER

Even a tea-drinking household can use a coffee grinder, which may double as a spice mill. Just be sure to clean it after each use—unless, of course, you prefer a little essence of cloves in your Morning Blend.

basics

knives and cutting boards

CHEF'S KNIFE

Its long, hefty blade measures anywhere from eight to fourteen inches and neatly chops vegetables and slices through meat; its flat side can be used to smash garlic or transfer ingredients to the pan.

PARING KNIFE

A paring knife with a three- to four-inch blade cuts fruit beautifully; its compact size and extra-sharp point give you the leverage you need to penetrate hard-to-cut foods.

SERRATED KNIFE

A serrated knife (eight inches on average) is indispensable for slicing bread, tomatoes, and other slightly soft foods. The "teeth" on the blade gently ease their way into the food, giving you seamless slices. (A flat blade would make a mess of things.)

CUTTING BOARD

Wooden boards are ideal cutting surfaces because they have a little "give" to them, allowing the knife to do all the work. Plastic boards can dull knives more quickly over time, although they are easier to clean and maintain. Good-quality plastic cutting boards can be placed in the dishwasher, whereas wooden ones cannot; the latter also need to be oiled periodically (use walnut oil) and kept dry to prevent cracking.

organization

easy access

The most sensible kitchen setup keeps frequently used tools and appliances within reach.

rails and racks

INSTALL A chrome rail positioned above your stove keeps your cooking utensils accessible and in a neat row. Hung from the kitchen ceiling, a heavy-duty cast-iron rack holds the pots and pans you cook with most.

counters

DISPLAY If you have lots of counter space and cook frequently, there's no reason to hide your small appliances: You'll just keep diving into cabinets to retrieve them. Attractive toasters and toaster ovens, blenders, food processors, coffee grinders, and coffeemakers can stay on the counter.

STOW AWAY Keep special-occasion appliances, such as a waffle iron, out of sight: Even a large kitchen can make better use of the space they take up. If you have little counter space, you will need to be more rigorous about what's accessible, which might mean stowing the blender after each use.

knife storage

PROTECT An in-drawer or countertop knife block protects your blades best. Opt for an in-drawer knife block rather than storing knives individually in plastic sleeves, which fall apart over time. Never toss your knives haphazardly into a drawer: You increase the chances of cutting yourself and damaging the blades.

It's 8 P.M. Do you know where your ice-cream bowls are? You'll find them in seconds if you reorganize the contents of your cabinets and cupboards, both above- and below-counter. It will take only an hour or so, and will save you much more time in the long run.

storage

cabinets and cupboards

TAKE INVENTORY Start by pulling everything out and placing the items on a large table.

ORGANIZE Put pots, pans, and bowls into groups and create a loose hierarchy based on how often you use the pieces. (Donate near duplicates or anything you know you'll never use to charity.)

REARRANGE Organize your cupboards with access in mind: More frequently used and heavier items should be within easy reach. Any that are rarely used but have some heft to them, such as a fondue pot, should go toward the back of a midlevel shelf.

THINK LOGICALLY Consider how the items are used: Those for cooking and food preparation should be kept in cabinets near the stove and work surfaces; those for eating should be closer to the sink, refrigerator, and dishwasher.

ASSIGN Breakable and/or valuable pieces can go on a shelf that's out of children's reach, or you can add child-proof latches to the cabinet doors.

HANG Small-scale metal grids, which attach to the wall or to the inside of a cupboard door, are useful for hanging small kitchen tools that get tangled up in kitchen drawers.

shelves

ATTACH Plastic-coated wire undershelf bins and freestanding stacking units will nearly double your storage space.

INSTALL Shelf-level bins—on gliders or not—will organize contents further.

organization

To maximize the space in your drawers and behind your cabinet doors, you'll need to minimize: Throw things out, and give things away. Just because your pots and pans are out of sight doesn't mean they have to be out of control.

flatware drawers

INSTALL Drawer dividers and utensil trays (large enough to accommodate any oversize pieces) will keep your kitchen accoutrements in order.

INSERT Flatware trays come in many variations, so make sure to choose one that fits comfortably in your drawer. Dividers and trays are usually made of either plastic or metal, each with its pitfalls. Plastic collects dust more easily, whereas utensils and flatware are more likely to get stuck in wire baskets.

storage drawers

STACK Pots and pans should be grouped by like kind and placed one inside the other, from smallest to largest. If you have room, it's best to keep lids atop their pots or pans; otherwise, arrange them from smallest to largest and keep their partners close by.

under the kitchen sink

STREAMLINE In the cabinet space under your sink, take advantage of plastic organizers, including a pull-out trash can on gliders and door attachments that hold sponges, brushes, and plastic wrap and aluminum foil.

CORRAL Place all cleaning supplies in a caddy or bucket (or two) that can be pulled out when you need them.

what goes where

It's always daunting to take on an appliance that dwarfs you, but remember that your refrigerator and freezer already have compartments that you can adapt as needed. If you plan your storage strategy section by section, you'll never have to search for anything, and nothing will go to waste.
STORE Some plastic storage bags and containers are designed specifically for freezing. The best of these are either sealable or relatively flat to keep out excess air and moisture and lock in freshness. Containers can be easily labeled and stacked.
ARRANGE Perishable foods should go at the bottom and toward the back of the refrigerator, not on the door; the latter sees too much action and fluctuation in temperature. This means butter and eggs go inside, even if the refrigerator has specific compartments for them on the door. (And eggs should always be kept in their original cartons, which help preserve them.)
DESIGNATE The lower shelf, where it's coldest, is best for dairy products. Produce does indeed stay fresher in a crisper drawer, which has a slightly higher humidity level than the rest of the refrigerator. As for the door, use it to store bottled food and condiments that don't spoil quickly.

longevity

Generally, a *sell-by* date on a package means that its contents are safe to consume for about a week thereafter; a *use-by* date means you're tempting fate if you wait three days or more before consuming. Bear in mind, these dates refer to safety, not freshness.

IN A 40°F REFRIGERATOR

Item	How long it lasts
Butter	2 months
Cheese, hard	6 months
Cheese, soft and opened	10 days
Cheese, soft and unopened	3 weeks
Eggs, hard-cooked	1 week
Eggs, uncooked in shell	1 month
Fish, fresh	1 day
Greens	2 days
Meat, cooked	3 days
Meat, raw	3 days
Poultry, cooked	3 days
Poultry, fresh	2 days
Vegetables	3 days
White wine, recorked	2 days
White wine, vacuum-stopped	10 days

IN A 0°F FREEZER

Item	How long it lasts
Bread	3 months
Butter	9 months
Fish, fatty	3 months
Fish, lean	6 months
Fruit	9 months
Fruit juices	10 months
Hamburger, fresh	4 months
Ice cream/sorbet	2 months
Poultry, cooked	5 months
Poultry, uncooked	9 months
Steaks, uncooked	9 months
Vegetables	6 months

refrigerator
and freezer

the pantry

For the most part, foods with a long shelf life belong—you guessed it—on shelves. That may mean in kitchen cupboards or, if you have one, a pantry. Flour, sugar, spices, and unopened condiments can safely be kept in a pantry for a year or so. Canned foods belong in the pantry, too: They often last indefinitely but are best when consumed within a year. Pantries can be a real luxury for a serious cook, but it's important to know how to use one properly. Here's how to make it a kitchen cure-all instead of a catch all.

organization

arranging food

HEAVIER ITEMS Canisters of flour, bottles of cooking oil, and common canned foods should be at waist level for minimal hefting. Canned foods should be stacked neatly on lower shelves with labels facing you.

LIGHTWEIGHT ITEMS High shelves are better for breakfast cereals and boxes of pasta.

leftover space

If you still have room in your pantry after stocking it with food, consider delegating an area at the rear to little-used pans and appliances, such as Dutch ovens and fondue pots—you'll be surprised at how much space you gain in your kitchen. The same goes for infrequently used, delicate glassware: Place it on a high shelf and arrange pieces by size—small in front, taller in back. They'll be easier to reach and less likely to break.

cleaning supplies

Install hooks and pegs on every available inch of the pantry door to hold brooms, mops, aprons, spice racks, etc. If retrieving items is difficult, invest in a collapsible step stool that you can fold and hang on the back of the door or tuck into a recessed space.

storage containers

GLASS CONTAINERS Ideal for storing food, they can be microwaved, refrigerated, and cleaned in a dishwasher, and can often be reheated in an oven (some have a heat threshold of 400° F, so check the label). The downside is that they are breakable and sometimes heavy to lug to the kitchen counter; if you opt for them, make sure they have airtight rubber seals to lock in freshness.

PLASTIC CONTAINERS These are excellent for storing pastas, beans, flour, sugar, and salt. It's worth splurging on the best, because many inferior plastic containers are susceptible to stains and can warp with multiple exposure to dishwashers. The best are made of impact-resistant polycarbonate, which is particularly well suited for freezing and can withstand the heat and force of a dishwasher. Never use flimsy containers from grocery deli sections for long-term food storage—they are not airtight enough and are often made of substandard materials. See-through plastic boxes are ideal for putting away objects you're always reaching for, such as lightbulbs.

BASKETS Table linens, particularly napkins, look good folded and filed in low wicker baskets, which ultimately frees up valuable storage space in the kitchen and/or dining room.

spices and recipes

No one likes to eat the same thing day after day. As long as they're accessible, spices and recipes add variety to life in the kitchen.

spices

STORE Put them in carefully labeled, airtight tins or jars (you can buy spice kits, or devise your own system using recycled tins or jars).

SHELVE Place tins in a lidded box on a pantry shelf and jars in a spice rack on a cupboard or pantry door or shelf.

SMALL AMOUNTS Buy spices in minute quantities—chances are you won't use them up before their flavor starts to wane.

recipes

If your loose clippings look like something from the National Archive, it's time to devise a personal recipe book to keep them in order.

STEP 1 First, toss any recipe that is more than a year old and that you haven't tried yet—chances are, you'll never make it.

STEP 2 Arrange the remaining recipes by specific categories and subcategories, such as ingredients (vegetables, etc.) or type of dish (salads).

STEP 3 Tape or paste them onto paper, and place each page in a plastic sleeve inside three-ring binders with tabbed category dividers. The plastic sleeves will allow you to read the recipes while cooking and keep them splatter-free. Add in old-fashioned recipe cards, photographs of dishes, and your own notations.

STEP 4 Label the spine of your recipe book and file it with the rest of your cookbooks.

Your standard, everyday cookbooks should be easily accessible but not in danger of damage from grease or excessive heat; keep them on a shelf as far from the stove as possible. Do not store rare, precious, and/or rarely used cookbooks in the kitchen at all; instead, keep them on a bookshelf in your library or living room or in storage containers.

simple solutions

KITCHEN SHEARS

Your kitchen shears can do more than snip herbs: Use them to chop canned tomatoes, too. To avoid splatter, pour the tomatoes into a glass bowl or Pyrex measuring cup before cutting.

NONSTICK MEASURING

Syrups and oils usually stick to measuring spoons and cups, leaving your recipes shortchanged. Before measuring, run spoons and cups under hot water to keep the ingredients from sticking.

ICE CUBES

Rejuvenate stale, unsliced loaves of hearty bread by rubbing ice cubes across the top to dampen, then tossing the bread in a 375° F oven for about ten minutes.

FLAT ZESTERS

In addition to grating citrus zest, use flat zesters (also called rasps, graters, and microplanes) to mince garlic.

INSTANT SANDWICH PRESS

Instead of buying a sandwich maker, put a heatproof dinner plate and a twenty-eight-ounce can of vegetables on top of your buttered sandwich as it cooks in a frying pan over medium heat.

SALAD SPINNERS

Use your salad spinner not just to dry freshly washed greens but also to distribute dressing evenly on a prepared salad. It's less messy than tossing, and you won't use as much dressing.

HANDHELD GRATERS

If you don't have a strainer, simply squeeze citrus fruit over a handheld grater, which will keep seeds and flesh out of your juice.

WHITE VINEGAR

Eradicate mineral deposits from a stainless-steel pot by filling it with water and a half cup of white vinegar. Bring to a boil and simmer for an hour.

PAPER TOWELS

Use paper towels to spread butter in a pan or on a cookie sheet before baking, then simply discard them. Cut and shaped into a cone, they also function as emergency coffee filters.

HOMEMADE COPPER POLISH

Mix equal parts of salt and flour and add a few drops of white vinegar to make a paste. Use to polish copper bowls and pots.

DENTAL FLOSS

Goat cheese is always difficult to slice with a knife. Instead, use unwaxed, unflavored dental floss to make perfect disks. Floss is also good for slicing moist cakes and hard-cooked eggs.

COOKING OIL

A few drops of cooking oil will remove adhesive stickers from new purchases. Just rub with a soft cloth and rinse. (A dab of toothpaste mixed with the oil is even more effective.)

the
dining
room

The dining room is a land of opportunity. But all too often, it's left as uncharted territory—visited two or three times a year for holiday dinners and otherwise kept in museum condition, along with the goblets and china you're afraid to touch, let alone use. It's time, then, to stake your claim on the dining room's everyday use: Think of it as an *eating* room, the center of your home, where family and friends can gather over casual meals as well as formal ones. While that china and those starched linens have their moments, a few simple touches and table arrangements will imbue the room with practicality— and prettiness. And there's an added benefit supper in the kitchen just can't match: You can enjoy your meal with the waiting dirty dishes completely out of sight.

basics

TABLE
The ideal height for a dining room table is about thirty inches, which provides ample legroom underneath and keeps food within reach. A table's material—wood, metal, glass—is a matter of personal choice. Each has its own requirements for cleaning and up-keep. Tables that expand (with gate legs or leaves) are excellent for small dining spaces.

CHAIRS
Dining room chairs should have an approximate seat height of eighteen inches and a depth of sixteen inches, so that diners can sit at the table comfortably. It's always wise to purchase at least two extra dining chairs for the table so you can accommodate a larger crowd when needed.

LINENS
Even the neatest diner will make a mess of things at some point. Paper napkins are fine for family, but cloth will elevate any meal and should always be used for guests. Table-cloths, place mats, and runners are always helpful in protecting the surface of the table.

CERAMIC SERVING PIECES
Make sure to have an array of stackable serving dishes for main courses and sides. White pieces will blend in with nearly everything; they should be light enough to pass around the table.

SERVING UTENSILS
Always have a set of basic serving utensils on hand. These can include a variety of stainless-steel, wood, or even attractive plastic serving spoons, tongs, spatulas, and forks. In a pinch for a casual dinner, two wooden spoons ordinarily used for cooking and baking can become make-shift salad servers.

essentials for any meal

DINNER PLATES
A set of simple white ceramic plates that are dishwasher-, oven-, and microwave-safe is the best investment. Expensive china is wonderful for special occasions but may not always be dishwasher-safe.

STAINLESS-STEEL FLATWARE
A set of dishwasher-safe forks, knives, and soup and dessert spoons with little or no embellishment can be versatile, durable, and easy to replace when necessary.

SERRATED STEAK KNIVES
Keep a set for cutting beef or other dense cuts of meat; they'll handily slice bread and tomatoes as well.

DRINKING GLASSES
Whether they hold water, milk, juice, or a cocktail, they shouldn't be too dainty for an adult or too daunting for a young child. The simpler the design, the more likely they will match the rest of your table.

WINEGLASSES
Cabernet vs. Chablis? Figuring out which glass is appropriate for reds and whites can be confusing, so get yourself a set of medium-size wine-glasses for everyday sipping. Humble glass tumblers are another casual alternative.

You seldom use that inherited bone china/linen table-cloth/crystal glass set, because you're sure you'll break or stain half of it in a clumsy moment. A few careful steps can prevent both accidents and heartache.

fragile pieces

CLEAN Wash wineglasses and fine-china cups and saucers immediately after use, and make sure they are bone-dry before storing them.

STORE Arrange items in specially padded storage containers with zippered lids. (For extra protection, wrap them individually in acid-free tissue paper first.)

STOW Place the containers on high shelves in a kitchen or hall closet or the pantry, or in a dining room sideboard or cabinet.

flatware

ARRANGE If you have enough drawer space in a dining room sideboard or buffet, array your flatware singly in rows according to type: salad forks, dinner forks, knives, soup spoons, dessert spoons, etc. You will instantly be able to assess and access your stock whenever you need it.

CONDENSE If you are short on drawer space, stack like items of flatware within a compartmentalized drawer insert. Expandable plastic inserts are preferable to fixed wooden ones, because they are easily cleaned and can accommodate larger pieces, such as serving spoons. Never use metal mesh inserts: Silverware tends to get stuck (and damaged) in them.

tablecloths

STACK After laundering tablecloths, arrange them neatly on shelves in a sideboard or buffet, or on high shelves in a kitchen or hall closet or the pantry. Those that are used more frequently should go at the top of the pile for easy retrieval.

LABEL If your tablecloths are quite similar, save for a delicate scalloped edge or lace detail, attach handwritten labels to them for quick identification. Including measurements on the labels will save you time when you're ready to set the table.

CANDLE

If your silverware drawer sticks each time you try to open it, rub the point where it meets the runner with a candle. It should slide out easily.

DISH TOWEL

To add immediate pizzazz to an ordinary meal, use a colorfully striped dish towel (placed sideways, not lengthwise) as a decorative table runner.

PAPER TOWELS

If you don't have zippered storage containers, stack china with a few paper towels between each piece to protect it from breakage.

ADDED COLOR

Give everyday white tableware a boost by accessorizing with floral linens and smaller pieces with colorful glazes.

FLOATING CENTERPIECE

Rather than sticking flowers in a vase, float petals and buds in a wide, shallow container of water along with a few votive candles.

PILLOW TALK

A sturdy coffee table and comfy throw pillows can substitute for a dining table when you're having an informal meal.

the
bedroom

The bedroom is your refuge from the world, the place where you spend a third of your life, where your day begins and ends. This is one of the few rooms in the house where you can let both fantasy and function help you create a personal haven. Indulge yourself with sheets, pillows, comforters, curtains, flowers, scented candles— whatever will help you feel completely comfortable. You'll appreciate it all as you start the morning refreshed and, after a hard day's work, as you ease into a relaxing night.

BED

Beds come in any number of shapes and sizes, but no matter what you choose, you'll need a strong frame. Four-poster, no-poster, canopy, headboard, footboard: These are entirely personal choices, although the headboard should be tall enough to offer back support if you like to sit up in bed and read. As for a bed's overall size, it should neither dwarf the room nor be dwarfed by it.

DRESSER

A dresser is essential in a bedroom, particularly if closet space is scarce. It should be sturdily constructed, suit your decor, and ideally have multiple drawers in varying sizes to accommodate clothing of different types. Dressers with built-in inserts (or even a removable tray) for arranging delicate items are especially desirable, as are those that come with a matching mirror, although you can always add store-bought inserts and provide your own attractive mirror. If you don't have the wall space for a large, wide dresser, consider investing in two tall, skinny ones that will provide equal storage without taking up so much room.

NIGHT TABLE

In addition to adding character to your bedroom, night tables (also called bedside tables or nightstands) provide you with valuable space—both on their top surfaces and on shelves and in drawers—for anything from a clock radio to a contact-lens case. Ideally, the tables should stand between sixteen and twenty-five inches tall, or no higher than six inches from the top of the mattress, so that you can reach them easily while lying down. Position them close to the bed, but not so close that you'll have difficulty making the bed.

BEDSIDE LAMPS

Even if you don't like to read in bed, you'll be grateful for a pair of bedside lamps when you're trying to find a tissue in the middle of the night. Table lamps, which rest on a night table next to the bed, should be positioned to cast light directly where it's needed (such as on the pages of a book). Wall-mounted sconces come in two basic versions—swing-arm and stationary—and free up precious table space. Swing-arm sconces should be mounted about a foot and a half above the top of the mattress and centered above bedside tables, while a stationary sconce should be mounted at the same height but can be positioned a bit closer to the bed.

UPHOLSTERED ARMCHAIR

An armchair is not absolutely necessary in a bedroom, but it's nice to have a comfortable piece of furniture to sink into while reading or enjoying a cup of tea. A chair in the bedroom can be useful as well: It's convenient to have a chair to sit on while removing your shoes or getting dressed. It's also a logical place to toss extra bed throws and decorative pillows before you retire for the night.

five easy pieces

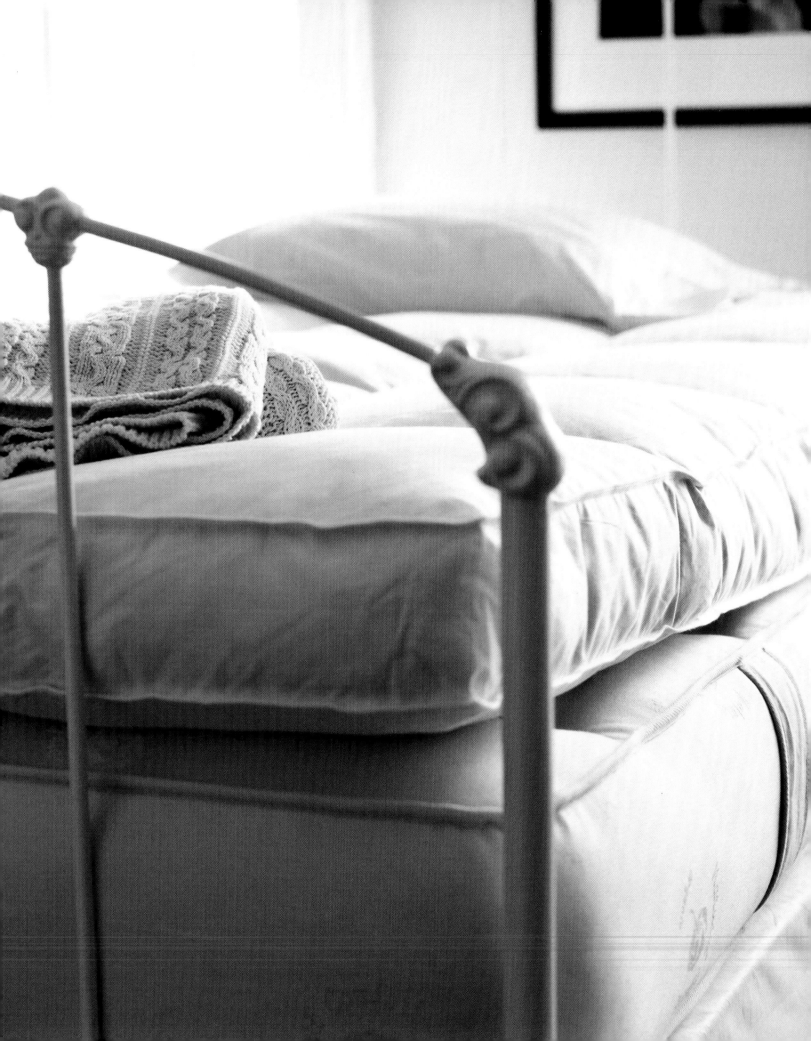

MATTRESS

Today's box springs are almost universally constructed of coil springs within a wood framework covered by fabric ticking. Mattresses, which go on top, are made with any number of materials, including coils, foams, and feathers. To assess comfort in a mattress, test several before buying one. A good barometer: It should feel comfortably soft on your joints but also provide ample support. In other words, you shouldn't sink or sag, but neither should you lie straight as a board. (A long warranty period is another benchmark of a quality mattress.) Mattresses used to commonly measure six to eight inches thick, but many are now being produced at thicknesses of up to twenty inches, which poses problems for anyone who wants to buy sheets in standard sizes. For additional comfort, try a foam or a synthetic- or natural-fiber mattress pad on top of the mattress. Some mattresses now even come with built-in foam or feather padding, known as a pillowtop. These can all be used with a mattress cover, although some pads are designed with attached sheeting that fits around the mattress, making a separate mattress cover unnecessary.

PILLOWS

A pillow should support your neck and help it stay aligned with your spine to prevent stiffness while you sleep. If you sleep on your side, you'll need more support; people who sleep on their stomachs or backs need less. Many manufacturers now produce pillows in varying degrees of firmness, which is helpful if you know how much support you need. Pillows can have fillings of feathers, down, a mix of down and feathers, natural fibers such as wool and cotton, foam and other man-made materials such as synthetic down, and other assorted elements. Wool and cotton tend to flatten over time and stay that way, but good-quality down can be easily fluffed up again. Let your personal preferences guide you. Feathers and down, of course, are generally ill-advised for people with allergies, although some down fillers are subjected to high-tech cleaning processes that rid them of most allergens. Pillow covers, which zip shut directly over pillows, provide an extra layer of protection under pillowcases; anyone sensitive to allergens (including dust mites) should buy the hypo-allergenic variety.

bedding

basics

linens

SHEETS

There's a reason 100 percent cotton sheets are ubiquitous: No other material works as well. Cotton-polyester sheets tend to pill and lack the "breathability" of pure cotton; silk sheets are expensive and require dry-cleaning; linen sheets can be costly and initially feel rough, although the fibers eventually soften after repeated washing. Much has been made in recent years of the thread counts of cotton sheets—mostly by savvy marketing strategists. Thread-count numbers stand for the number of threads per square inch, and some sheets that have 400 or more certainly feel great to the touch. However, a high thread count doesn't guarantee longevity or even quality; it's the fiber that ultimately counts. Look for sheets made with pima or Egyptian combed cotton; a 200-thread-count sheet in these cottons will feel more than luxurious on any bed. Because mattress sizes vary greatly, it's sometimes advisable to buy a larger flat sheet that can be folded and tucked around a plus-size mattress in lieu of a fitted bottom sheet. Some people who sleep with a comforter inside a duvet cover skip the flat top sheet entirely.

COMFORTERS

Comforters, like pillows, come in a variety of materials, such as down, synthetic down, cotton, wool, and silk. In this case, it's necessary to decide how much weight you want on top of you while you sleep and how warm you want to be. Comforters filled with down and wool keep you warm and wick away moisture, but you probably won't want them on your bed in the middle of the summer. Cotton, on the other hand, doesn't insulate as well, but it is a good warm-weather alternative, as is silk. The down equivalent of cotton's thread count is fill power: A fill power of 550 to 800 ensures fluffier, softer, warmer, and more durable down; a cotton shell with a thread count of 230 or higher will keep the down from escaping easily. Blankets and quilts, of course, are still reliable stand-bys, but they often weigh more than comforters and require a flat sheet to separate them from the sleeper—even the softest wool blanket isn't soft enough to sleep under without a protective sheet. Coverlets and bedspreads add decorative interest to a bedroom but are usually turned down at night or removed from the bed.

Having a disorganized mess at your bedside is more nightmare than night table. The best way to arrange it is to assess what you want on it and/or inside it. You'll also want to make sure your dresser drawers are in order. If you do not have adequate bedroom closet space, you'll need to take extra care in organizing them.

night tables

DISPLAY What belongs in plain sight is what looks good and what makes sense: An alarm clock, reading glasses, a water carafe and/or glass, a vase, a book (or a small stack of books), and small framed photographs all fit the bill.

HIDE If your night table has a drawer, stock it with the unglamorous accoutrements: eye pillows and eye masks, earplugs, lip balm, hand and foot creams.

PUT AWAY If you must watch television from bed (keeping in mind that a barrage of visual stimuli tends to make the brain more active and discourage restful sleep), toss the remote in the drawer before turning out the light.

SELECT If you like to have a telephone on your night table, choose a demure, preferably cordless model; a hulking one will remind you of work, not relaxation, and take up valuable real estate.

dresser drawers

ORGANIZE Dressers typically have smaller drawers at the top and larger ones at the bottom. Underwear belongs in top drawers; heavier garments go in bottom ones.

MAXIMIZE To make the most of drawer space, install plastic dividers, which are especially helpful in organizing small items, such as underwear, bras, and socks or stockings. (Wood dividers can snag clothing.)

organization

extra storage

If your bed frame is raised off the floor, consider the area underneath it for storage. It's particularly handy if you have limited closet or dresser space for clothes you wear only seasonally, such as thick wool sweaters and shoes or winter boots.

under the bed

STORE Storage containers and boxes made of plastic, canvas, and wood are most desirable (some even have wheels for easy retrieval), although each has its particular foibles. Other oversize or cumbersome objects under the bed, such as luggage and cold-weather blankets and comforters, should be kept in large plastic containers for extra protection.

SELECT If you choose wood boxes, opt for cedar, which helps deter moths, and line it with plain unbleached muslin to counter the wood's acidity. Add cedar drawer liners (or blocks) to plastic and canvas boxes, and use canvas for delicate items such as cashmere sweaters, which need circulating air.

REVISIT Even if you use top-notch storage containers under the bed, it's important to check them periodically and reassess their contents. Could that winter comforter use a good shaking out or cleaning before you put it to use? Would those sweaters be better off with a fresh stock of cedar blocks? Also, anything kept in tight plastic containers should be aired out at least every six months.

CLEAN "Out of sight, out of mind" rarely applies when it comes to your home. Just because you have room to stow things under your bed doesn't mean you are exempt from cleaning the space itself. At least once a month, remove storage boxes and suitcases and give the floor (and rug or carpet, if applicable) a thorough cleaning.

the clothes closet Who hasn't fantasized about having a movie-star closet, the kind with storage for hundreds of shoes, row upon row of dresses and gowns, and dozens of neatly folded cashmere sweaters? But even if your bedroom closet isn't the stuff of dreams, you can squeeze more space out of it and make it function more smoothly by employing a few simple tricks and a handful of inexpensive tools. Take a good, hard look at your wardrobe, assess your storage needs, consider which organizational devices will work best for you, and open the door to a brilliant new closet— whether you're a movie star or not.

basics

five organizing essentials

CLOTHING ROD

The most effective clothing rod is made of chrome or heavy-duty aluminum and can withstand the weight of all your hanging clothes. A rod bolted into the wall is preferable to one fitted into separate wall mounts. A wooden clothing rod will become worn with frequent use, and hangers will not slide easily along it.

STORAGE BOXES

Unless you live year-round in the tropics (or inside the Arctic Circle), you will probably need storage boxes for clothes that you wear in only one season, or for special occasions. Keep them on high shelves in your closet, in closets elsewhere in the house, or under the bed.

SHELVES AND DRAWERS

Your closet can't hold everything. Sweaters and other delicate knits, T-shirts, and accessories can go on shelves or in drawers. If you don't have dresser space, baskets or containers on shelves can hold underwear, socks, T-shirts, and workout gear. A set of inexpensive hanging canvas shelves can also easily be suspended from a clothing rod and provide very useful space.

SHOE ORGANIZER

A shoe organizer is essential for any well-run clothes closet. A shoe rack, placed on the closet floor, is suitable for anything with a heel but less handy for flat-heeled sneakers and boots, which can dislodge easily and slide off. A hanging canvas or plastic shoe organizer is like a vertical stack of shoe boxes: Pairs are tucked into individual recesses and easily retrieved. See-through plastic shoe boxes protect shoes from dust.

GARMENT BAG

A sturdy cloth garment bag protects suits, dresses, and jackets better than plastic (leather, in particular, is susceptible to cracking if kept in plastic). Remove clothes from dry-cleaning plastic the minute you get home and hang your clothes on proper hangers. Return the wire hangers to the dry cleaner for reuse.

five hangers

BASIC

A basic wooden hanger provides enough support for a shirt, as will a tubular plastic hanger.

ALL-PURPOSE

An all-purpose wooden hanger, which includes a felt-lined clamp, is designed for trousers, skirts, and both pieces of a suit.

NOTCHED

A notched wooden hanger has indentations at the shoulder in which the straps of a dress or inner loops of dress pants can nestle, preventing the item from slipping off.

DELUXE

A deluxe wooden or plastic hanger has widened shoulders intended to keep a jacket in good shape.

PADDED

A padded fabric hanger is designed for delicate dresses and gowns. It retains their shape along the shoulder and keeps the garments from slipping.

organization

You may not need every storage device ever invented, but chances are you can benefit from many. Likewise, there is no one way to organize a space, but some schemes are better than others. Consider your storage needs and be realistic about the space you have to work with (measure carefully), and a plan will fall into place.

space

EVALUATE While there are many ways to maximize the space within your clothes closet—from install-it-yourself devices found at home-accessories stores to complete retrofitting by a professional designer—your closet needs to be properly measured first. Start by measuring your space carefully (to the nearest sixteenth-inch) before buying any hardware, such as rods and shelving units.

clothing rods

HEIGHT The right clothing rods can maximize the space within your closet. If you have a closet with a ceiling height of at least seven and a half feet, you will have room for two rods (one hung about three or four feet above the other). A clothing rod should hang at least forty-two inches above the floor, so that clothes will not touch the floor and you will be able to reach them easily.

DEPTH A rod should be positioned at least a foot from the back wall, if possible. (Ideally, the ends of your hangers will be at least three inches from the wall.)

ONLY ONE ROD If possible, reserve room in part of your closet for a single rod, from which pants, coats, and shoe organizers or canvas shelving units can be hung without hitting the floor or the lower rod.

shelves

CONTENTS Leave some space in your closet for shelves, which are crucial for holding delicate knits (or any clothing that will stretch out of shape on a hanger), accessories (bags and purses), storage boxes, or shoes.

DEPTH Shelves should be open and never deeper than fourteen inches—otherwise you'll have to fish around for what should really be close at hand.

MATERIAL Wooden shelves look nice and provide optimal support, although many metal and plastic-coated wire shelving units are on the market. (Note: Wire shelving tends to "rib" your clothing.) Acids in wooden shelves, including cedar, can deteriorate fabric, so line them with shelf paper or unbleached, undyed washed muslin, which is sold at fabric stores.

ALTERNATIVE If you don't want to buy expensive custom shelving or are tight on space, consider relegating some of the length of your clothing rod to accommodate hanging canvas shelves.

drawers

BITS AND PIECES Drawers—whether they are mounted to a wall or part of a tall lingerie chest that can be positioned inside the closet—help you organize small pieces such as underwear and accessories.

JEWELRY Drawers are also convenient for jewelry if you'd rather not keep it on top of a dresser in the bedroom proper.

OTHER OPTIONS If installing a set of drawers is too costly or complicated, substitute a set of baskets and place them on shelves.

doors

HINGES Hinged full-swing or bifold doors will allow you complete access to your closet, whereas dual-hung sliding doors prevent access to the center of the space. If every inch counts, consider replacing sliding doors with hinged ones.

organization

hanging clothes

There's no real use in organizing a closet filled with too many clothes you don't wear. First, you must pare down your wardrobe. Then sort your clothes by your daily clothing routine.

elementary editing

EVALUATE Take a look at your clothes and assess which you wear most, least, or not at all, keeping in mind that most people routinely wear only 20 percent of the clothes they own. (If you are completely overhauling your closet, remove everything from it and arrange clothing in like piles before you start editing.)

PURGE If you haven't worn an item in a year or more, or if the item no longer fits or is laughably out of date, give it to charity. If it's severely damaged, toss it out.

organize what is on your hangers

SORT Pulling together outfits will be much simpler if you group clothing by type: shirts, tops, skirts, pants, and suits. Then order them by both color and heft of fabric: from light to dark, lightweight to heavy.

ASSESS Consider the density of garments before hanging them on the rod. On average, a jacket or suit requires two to four inches of rod space; shirts, skirts, and pants need one to two inches; dresses, one to three inches; and overcoats and other bulky outerwear, four to six inches.

SPACE OUT Leave breathing room between garments— at least $1/4$ inch if possible, with fabrics barely grazing one another. Again, seasonality and frequency of use can be a big factor in delegating space: That taffeta evening gown in the roomy garment bag may have to be stored somewhere else.

organization

**folded clothes
and accessories**

It's often the small clothing items and accessories that make the biggest mess in a closet. Here's how to minimize it and use every inch of your closet.

folding clothes

CONTAIN When organizing folded sweaters, take care to place heavier sweaters at the bottom of the pile, and lighter ones, such as thin-ply cashmere, at the top; the same topple-proofing strategy applies to T-shirts and other pullover garments.

ORGANIZE After folding, arrange garments by function (athletic socks together, dress socks together), color (white to nude to bright color to black), and type (thongs, bikini underwear, and boy-cut briefs).

shoes

EDIT If you are like most Americans, you have more shoes than available slots on a shoe rack or shoe organizer. Decide which shoes you wear most often and place them on your closet's rack (or organizer), then store the remaining pairs in labeled plastic boxes on a high shelf, in another closet, or under your bed.

STORE Some people prefer to keep shoes in their original cardboard boxes, but they will not protect shoes as well and can be easily dented (and therefore crush your shoes) if too much weight is placed on top of them. If you do choose to store your shoes this way, snap a Polaroid of each pair and staple it to the box so that you can quickly identify the box's contents.

accessories

HOOKS AND RACKS Store bags, belts, ties, scarves, and other accessories in plain sight on hooks or racks, which can be attached to the inside of your closet door.

SHELVES AND CONTAINERS Large purses and totes can also be placed on shelves, as can smaller baskets or boxes that contain just one type of accessory, such as scarves, although you will have to dig through them to find the piece you want.

simple solutions

CHEST OR BENCH

A chest or bench placed at the foot of your bed is both decorative and useful. It provides extra seating and can hold bedding and blankets. A pure-cedar or cedar-lined chest is a good choice because it will repel moths, if not actually kill them.

BEDSIDE RUG

Hardwood floors and thin carpets can be cold when you swing out of bed in the morning. Place a thick, plush rug at the side of your bed to cushion your step. It's perfectly acceptable to put a rug on top of a carpet—in fact, the combination can be quite attractive.

ROLLUP BLACKOUT SHADE

Even slightly see-through curtains won't provide you with the privacy you need or keep the early-morning sun out of late risers' eyes. One solution for the bedroom is to combine your favorite curtains with an inconspicuous rollup blackout shade, which can be lowered whenever you feel like it.

WAX PAPER

Rub clothing rods with wax paper so that hangers slide along them more easily.

RODS

Spare yourself the time and energy it takes to install a second clothing rod below an existing one. Instead, invest in one with special hardware that allows you to hang it from the original rod.

LIGHTS

If you don't like the thought or expense of electrical light in your clothes closet, install a battery-powered, press-on light on an interior wall.

VALET HOOKS

In addition to placing hooks on walls and closet doors to hold items, install a sturdy valet hook on the door or on the wall next to your closet. You'll be able to hang up pieces of your outfit as you dress.

PLASTIC SHOE BOXES

In addition to shoes, plastic shoe boxes and shoe drawers make terrific containers for other accessories, such as jewelry, gloves, and scarves.

BELTS

A hanger or wall bracket with hooks is a smart way to keep all your belts untangled and easily accessible.

SCENTED LINERS

Scented drawer liners and sachets are pure indulgences, but they keep clothes smelling fresh, especially garments you wear infrequently and therefore seldom launder. If you'd like to save money, scent your drawers with empty perfume bottles.

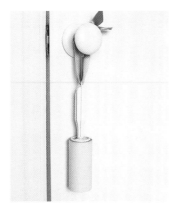

LINT BRUSHES

Keep a lint brush, a roller, or a depiller hanging from your closet door to remove whatever should not be attached to your sweater, pants, or blouse.

FABRIC SOFTENER

Stick fabric-softener sheets inside your shoes to keep them smelling fresh; also place sheets on closet shelves and in hampers and drawers.

the bathroom

You shower, brush your teeth, and put on your makeup in the bathroom each day, but that doesn't mean the space has to be strictly mundane. You can add plenty of personality to the bath, turning a room of humdrum function into an oasis of tranquillity and calm. Plush towels arranged in neat piles, an assortment of colorful bath oils and gels, and cotton balls piled high in a sea-shell, for example, will go a long way toward helping you feel refreshed and at ease. Rather than getting in and out as fast as you can, you'll want to soak it all in.

five easy pieces

CABINETS

Cabinets are ideal for hiding toiletries and bulk items such as toilet paper; the height of the items you store inside one should determine which shelf they go on. (Larger items such as hair dryers can be stored on a cabinet shelf or in a bin or drawer under the counter.)

MIRRORED MEDICINE CABINET

A mirrored medicine cabinet is invaluable in the bathroom. It holds toiletries and makeup, bandages and vitamins, toothpaste and emery boards, and more (provided there's no cascade every time it opens, of course). The bonus is the mirror: If your bathroom currently has no medicine cabinet but a gargantuan wall-mounted mirror instead, do not hesitate to replace the latter with the former. Opt for sconces mounted on either side of the cabinet instead of a mirror with attached lighting on top, which will cast unflattering light and shadows.

HOOKS

Affix hooks to the back of the bathroom door to hold bathrobes, clothing, and wet towels. A multi-hook unit can be hung over the top of the door without drilling.

TOWEL BARS, RINGS, AND KNOBS

Wherever you have wall space, consider installing a towel bar, ring, or knob. Your towels will dry much faster and be less likely to sour. While it's a decided luxury, an electric towel heater can be a godsend in a chilly, damp house. Never throw towels over the shower-curtain rod— they pick up grime and bacteria there.

SHOWER CADDY

A smart shower caddy includes trays for soap, bath sponges, and shampoo and also hooks for hanging a washcloth, a bath mitt, or anything suspended from a loop. Even if a shower caddy has supplemental suction-cup attachments, it should also fit tightly over a shower arm to avoid slipping (suction cups inevitably lose their grip on tile). Chrome and plastic-coated wire shower caddies hold up best; wood, plastic, and other metal ones attract gunk and rust, and fall apart easily.

basics

helpful additions

SHOWERHEAD

Why settle for a single-spray showerhead? Take the plunge and install a pivoting one with multiple spray options, from a fine mist to full-on drenching. You can make this change yourself in minutes—no plumber required.

COTTON TOWELS

Almost all bath towels sold in the United States are made of cotton terry cloth, although not all are plush. Some have a chemical finish that makes them feel fluffy in the store, but this coating wears away after a few washes and leaves your formerly plumped-up towel shockingly scratchy. A heavier towel isn't necessarily more absorbent, either; it's the quality of the fiber and the absorbency of the terry-cloth loops that matter. As with bedsheets, always look for towels made with high-quality cotton, such as Egyptian or pima.

BATH MAT

A bath mat is the best way to prevent puddles. Choose one in a cotton terry that matches your towels and can be washed easily. Another option: A sea-grass rug is attractive and comfortable underfoot, and it can be shaken out periodically to clean it.

TUB PILLOW

A terry-cloth tub pillow will help you relax even more as you soak. Better yet, apply a facial mask and let it do its work as you rest your head on the pillow.

CANDLES

Candles add a romantic touch to the bathroom, making it seem like a sanctuary. A row of votive candles—or stubby tapers and pillars salvaged from dinner parties—will cast everything in a soft glow. Avoid scented candles here: They'll interfere with perfumed soaps and bath oils.

organization

store and relax

Whether you're reaching for a Band-Aid (*ouch!*) or the bath salts (*ahhh!*), you need to know what's where.

shelves

STACK AND FOLD Most bathrooms don't have enough shelves, but if you're lucky enough to have a set, use them efficiently. Open shelves are most suitable for towels, which should be stacked in piles (hand towels in one pile, bath sheets in another). Try to keep them neatly folded; otherwise, your bathroom will look messy even if it's spotless.

storage containers

STOW If bathroom shelving space is limited, countertop baskets, bins, and boxes are helpful for corralling toiletries. If you have little room for stowing hand towels, you can roll them up and place them in a wicker or perforated metal basket.

RELOCATE Cotton swabs and cotton balls look much tidier when they're removed from their original packaging and placed in apothecary jars, or even just an attractive bowl or a deep seashell. The same goes for bath beads and bath salts.

tubside table

INDULGE If you have the space for it, a small tubside table can hold containers of bath salts, soaps, and scrub brushes. It's the bath lover's answer to a shower caddy.

the medicine cabinet

Bathroom organization is most critical in the medicine cabinet. If the cabinet is neat and orderly, chances are the rest of the bathroom will follow suit. Try these three steps to optimizing the space behind the mirror.

1. PURGE

Start your overhaul of the medicine cabinet by removing everything that's not vital to your daily life.

EDIT Throw out unwanted lipstick, nail polish that's gummed up beyond hope, frayed toothbrushes, bald emery boards, bent tweezers, stray bandages, and perfume you've always hated.

2. REGROUP

Gather like items into groups and assess how and where they should be placed.

GATHER Pull tubes of eyeliner and bottles of nail polish together; gather toothpaste, toothbrushes, and floss; introduce combs to brushes.

ALLOCATE Decide what is appropriate for the cabinet and what will do better in a drawer.

GROUP The shelf height in your cabinet may dictate which items go where, but as a general rule try to keep product families together.

3. RELOCATE

Makeup should obviously be kept in its original packaging for fast identification, but lone accessory pieces, such as nail clippers, files, emery boards, and tweezers, aren't likely to be misplaced if they're gathered in a cup. Hair clips, elastics, bobby pins, and rubber bands are easier to access in a single plastic container with a snap lid; toothbrushes and toothpaste take up less space if they are stored upright in a cup or a jar.

makeup makeover

When editing the contents of the medicine cabinet and/or makeup drawer, consider the age and the condition of your makeup and applicators. You'll probably end up tossing more than you think—and not feeling guilty about it.

WHEN IS THE RIGHT TIME TO TOSS?

Item	Time
Powder-based makeup	2 years
Eyeliner/mascara	3 months
Anything that smells "off" or is discolored	immediately
Liquid makeup that has separated into layers	immediately
Solid oil-based makeup that has droplets on it	immediately
Cracked eye shadows	immediately

MAINTENANCE

It's also important to keep makeup tubes and bottles and makeup applicators in top shape.

MASCARA WANDS If needed, clean them with tissue paper, not facial tissue, which will leave lint behind.

COTTON SWABS Dip them into makeup remover to clean around the necks of makeup tubes; use nail-polish remover to do the same with bottles of nail polish.

MAKEUP BRUSHES Use baby shampoo to wash them, then let them air-dry before returning them to the cabinet or drawer.

the linen closet

If you are fortunate enough to have a linen closet in the hallway outside your bathroom (or even inside the bathroom itself), make the most of it. By retrofitting the space to suit your needs, you can banish leaning towers of towels and tame the bedlam of bedsheets. Such sorting and stacking just might make room for some of the clutter from the bathroom drawers and the medicine cabinet (and maybe even some overflow from the kitchen and dining room). Opening the linen closet will no longer mean facing a tangle of terry cloth; instead, it will be an oasis of calm.

organization

assess your shelves

STACK Two big shelves in a standard eight-foot-high closet are not nearly enough. Sheets and towels are easier to organize (and less likely to topple) if they are arrayed in short stacks on multiple shelves.

MEASURE Rejiggering the height of your shelves will help you get more from your linen closet. Ten inches between shelves is good for sheets and table linens, twelve to sixteen inches for towels, and eighteen inches or more (measured from the ceiling) for the top shelf, for blankets and other seasonal items.

DIVIDE If your shelves are fixed at inconvenient levels and you don't want to take on the cost of reworking them, you can streamline the space by devising your own system of baskets, shelf dividers, and plastic-covered wire bins that attach to the underside of existing shelves.

stacking

SORT Divide your linens into categories—bed linens, table linens, towels. Then, subdivide by room: master bedroom, kids' bedrooms, guest bedroom, dining room, master bathroom, kids' bathroom, guest bathroom.

TAG Using adhesive tabs or just tape and slips of paper, label your shelves to reflect these groups, and store the items you use most frequently, such as towels and bed linens, on shelves at or near eye level. (Table linens, which don't see as much action, can be assigned to a higher or lower shelf.)

ROTATE Within each stack, place freshly laundered linens on top, and always take the set to be used next from the bottom. This rotation will keep linens from sitting too long and getting musty.

ALLOCATE Assigning different-colored linens to different rooms of the house, such as white for the master bedroom and bath and blue for guests' quarters, will help keep everything organized.

top shelf

Devote the top shelf to seasonal items like wool blankets and down comforters, and store them in zippered plastic cases (the original packaging, if you didn't throw it out). The top shelf is also well suited for special-occasion table linens, beach blankets, and towels.

floor

Use the space between the floor and the bottom shelf to store baskets, hampers, and small appliances, such as a handheld vacuum.

door

As with other rooms in the house, don't forget to use the back of the closet door. Attach hooks and baskets to hold such items as bathrobes, bath soap, toilet paper, lightbulbs, and scented sachets or bags of cedar chips.

alternative storage

If space is really tight, adhere to a strict daily-linens-only policy in the linen closet, and assign less frequently used linens to other areas of the house. Store table linens in a dining room sideboard or hutch; tuck guest linens into a dresser drawer in the guest bedroom (or hang them over a hanger in the closet).

first-aid kit and medicines

The hallway linen closet is an ideal spot for storing a first-aid kit as well as prescription and over-the-counter medicines. Stow first-aid kits and medicine on a high shelf, so children cannot get to them. You do not need to keep first-aid items in a standard-issue first-aid kit; a plastic organizer with a tight snap-on lid will do just fine.

STER BEDROOM

ELLA'S

PSTAIRS BATH

KIDS' BATH

MILK

There are hundreds of rejuvenating bath oils and salts on the market, but don't forget that milk in the bath both exfoliates and softens skin. Add two cups of fresh milk or one cup of powdered skim milk to bathwater for an inexpensive indulgence.

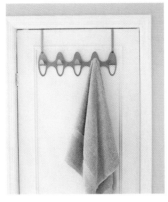

OVER-THE-DOOR HOOK

A multihook unit—slung over the top of the door rather than screwed into it—holds towels, robes, and washcloths.

OLD TOOTHBRUSH

To clean grout between tiles, get rid of gunk in a showerhead, polish the spot where the faucet meets the sink, and scour other difficult-to-reach crevices, use an old toothbrush. A battery-operated one practically does the work for you.

SQUEEGEE

Regularly wiping down shower doors and tub tile with a squeegee after showering or bathing will help prevent mildew and soapy scum from building up.

SHEET CHEAT

Sheet sets in constant disarray? Keep them together by placing freshly laundered and folded sheets within a matching pillowcase from the same set. Sheets will never get lost in the shuffle again.

SPACE-SAVING STORAGE

Vacuum storage bags will save you lots of shelf space. Simply place sheet sets inside, use the hose of your vacuum cleaner to suck out excess air, and stow.

J.H. DESIGN, INC.

the home office

THE HOME OFFICE Whether you work at home full-time or simply need a clean, organized spot for paying bills and balancing your checkbook, a home office can be a lifesaver. The room functions best (and *you* function best) when it's set up properly: Like any smart business plan, the design for your home office should focus on both your immediate needs and long-term goals. If you have visions of grandeur but are short on space, devise a strategy that will make the most of what you have and deliver better than expected results. If you have space to spare, allocate it for maximum efficiency. You'll soon find that doing business is always a pleasure in a home office that works.

10 Monday

Salvador Dali born 1904

11 Tuesday

Frank Stella born 1936
Katherine Hepburn born 1907

12 Wednesday

13 Thursday

Friday 14

Armed Forces Day

Saturday 15

Liberace born 1919
Henry Fonda born 1905

Sunday 16

June 04

S	M	T	W	T	F	S
		1	2	3	4	5
6	7	8	9	10	11	12
13	14	15	16	17	18	19
20	21	22	23	24	25	26
27	28	29	30			

PLEASE JOIN US FOR BRUNCH

DATE: SUNDAY, MAY 16TH

TIME: NOON

PLACE: THE MOORE'S

PLEASE R.S.V.P. BY MAY 13TH

Call the
Moores about
Brunch

DESK/WORKSTATION

Ideally, your desk or worktable will be at least five feet long and thirty inches deep, which should give you enough room for a computer as well as a telephone and a desktop organizer, and space for writing. Some desks on the market have keyboard trays in place of a pull-out drawer, so you lose drawer space but gain a place to type comfortably and stow the keyboard away from dust. For those who work full-time at home, an L-shaped desk provides even more room and a separate console for the computer; this configuration also keeps you from staring at the computer screen all day and reduces eyestrain.

COMPUTER STATION

If you don't have the space (or the taste) for an L-shaped desk, you may want to place your computer on a separate cart, preferably on wheels, so that you can bring it toward you when you want to work on it and put it aside when you don't. Make sure your cart will hold your computer monitor and related components, such as keyboard, mouse, and hard drive. Wheels that lock are also helpful in preventing the station from wobbling while you work. A laptop computer is obviously a great space saver and uses 90 percent less energy than its hulking desktop counterpart.

CHAIR

An office chair with some flexibility is most desirable: Its seat height, back, and armrests should be adjustable. The edge of the seat should curve so that it doesn't touch the backs of your knees and impede circulation. Chairs on wheels are helpful for moving from one spot to another at your workstation, although they don't do well on carpet with a deep pile. A standard seat height for a chair is about seventeen to eighteen inches, which means the height of your desk or workstation should be about twenty-eight or twenty-nine inches, with plenty of room for you to fit your knees under it while seated. You should also be able to place your feet completely flat on the floor while seated; otherwise, buy a footrest.

LIGHTING

A combination of overhead, ambient, and task lighting (a desk lamp) is best for the home office. Overhead light alone, depending on the position of your desk or workstation, often casts shadows or bounces off your computer screen, irritating your eyes and impeding your progress. But task lighting helps negate these effects while shedding better light on the workstation itself. Always position a desk lamp to the left or right of your computer screen rather than directly toward it; otherwise, the glare will tire your eyes.

SHELVING AND DRAWERS

Even one small shelf can be a boon to a home office: An item placed on it, such as a tray of unpaid bills, will not take up valuable desk space, but it won't be forgotten either. Shelves are also ideal for reference books, folders, and binders. Drawers, on the other hand, are better for items that you don't need to see all the time, such as supplies and stationery. Desktop organizers make useful containers for pencils, pens, and paper clips.

five easy pieces

basics

helpful additions

STAPLER
Still the best device for joining important papers together, condensing individual pieces of paper into categorized groups, and keeping pages of documents in proper order. Invest in a heavy-gauge spring-action model with a weighted bottom.

TAPE DISPENSER
Tape does everything, from sealing an envelope that has substandard adhesive, to repairing a tear on an important document, to affixing that cute snapshot of your dog to the front of your day planner.

PAPER CLIPS
A paper clip does the work of tape and staples but is less fixed, so you can separate documents as easily as you can join them. Paper clips come in myriad shapes and sizes, from standard-issue metal clips to plastic-coated wire ones.

BULLETIN BOARD
Out of sight, out of mind—unless your computer is on twenty-four hours a day and you routinely leave yourself reminders and to-do notes posted on the screen. Better to install a bulletin board near your desk to keep you from forgetting the important things.

PENCIL SHARPENER
You probably don't use a pencil as much as you once did, but it's still helpful for jotting down notes and doing quick arithmetic. If a large electric pencil sharpener takes up too much desk space, buy a tiny handheld one and stow it in a desk drawer or desktop organizer.

SCRATCH PAPER
Everybody needs to write something down once in a while. If you prefer not to use a system of notebooks, try keeping a small stack of scratch paper on hand, or adhesive-backed notepads, such as Post-it notes.

FILING SYSTEM
For some people, a file cabinet is necessary for organizing all their papers; for others, a desktop accordion file is sufficient. But every home office needs some sort of filing system for important documents. (You can't store your property deeds on your computer.)

SCISSORS
For cutting along the dotted line, not to mention making snowflakes or paper dolls in an idle moment.

PUSHPINS/TACKS
A bulletin board would be useless without them.

PEN
E-mail is usually but not universally appropriate. To write thank-you notes and the occasional personal letter, keep an old-fashioned ink pen on hand.

You've got wires tangling, lamplight glaring, and papers tumbling everywhere. What you need is a bit of good support.

electrical wiring

BIND To keep wires in a neat stream, tie them together loosely with plastic twist ties, cord clips, or cord bundles and tape them to the bottom of the desk, or attach them to plastic hooks that guide them to an outlet.

LABEL On pieces of tape or file labels, identify cords at both the source and the outlet, so you know what you're unplugging before it's too late.

GROUP Consolidate your plugs in a surge-protection strip, which can suppress spikes in electricity (and save you from losing data). Do not use a basic strip for computer components; it won't protect them from a power surge.

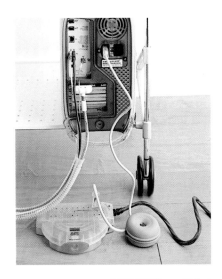

lighting

POSITION Arrange your monitor so that the ambient and task lighting complement each other: There should be no glare, reflection, or shadow cast on the computer screen.

VEIL Depending on the orientation of the room you use for your home office, you may also have to consider the effect of natural light coming in from windows and move the items on your desk accordingly, or use a curtain on the windows to diffuse bothersome light.

filing system

MAXIMIZE You will have to file papers, but how to file them is a matter of personal need and how much you want to spend. Short on space? A file cabinet on casters that can slide under your desk is a good option. Lots of room? Consider a variety of filing methods, such as accordion files, standing desktop files, file cabinets, and file boxes that can be placed on shelves.

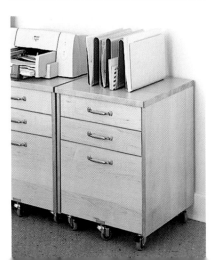

organization

mail

You've got many types of mail. You've also got many ways to deal with them.

the daily mail

SORT Go through your mail every day. If you let it pile up, it will become overwhelming.

PURGE Immediately throw out unwanted junk mail and credit-card solicitations (or put them through a shredder or rip them in half, if you're concerned about mail fraud).

FILE Place bills to be paid in your in box, put magazines and newspapers in a rack or periodical box, and file your banking and investment statements.

junk mail

MARK If you receive lots of junk mail, you can winnow it down. Check opt-out boxes on monthly statements so that companies will not sell your name and address, and call the National Opt Out Center (888-567-8688) to remove your name from major lists sold to direct-mail companies.

MAKE CALLS If you move, do not fill out a permanent change-of-address card from the U.S. Postal Service, which sells names; call companies individually or change your address on their monthly statements instead. If you are not interested in receiving catalogs, call the companies directly and insist that they stop sending them.

e-mail

SORT As with snail mail, e-mail can pile up, but if you go through it every day you can keep it manageable. Delete unwanted e-mail or spam (junk e-mail) immediately. If you routinely receive spam, forward it to uce@ftc.gov, which tracks spam e-mailers and devises ways to block them electronically. As for regular e-mails that you're not ready to delete, move them to folders with labels such as Meetings, Upcoming Events, Reports and Documents, etc.

filing

Too much information? Whether it's an important document, a receipt of purchase, or a magazine you can't bear to toss, sensible filing systems will keep the information you need at your fingertips—but out of sight.

the paper chase

BOX IT UP You can reduce mountains of paper to manageable molehills if you streamline and categorize them. Try keeping an attractive desktop file box at your workstation for all current papers and documents.

STORE When the papers are no longer needed for immediate reference, transfer them to another file box—such as a banker's box with a punch-out labeling system on the side—for archiving.

magazines and newspapers

EDIT Be ruthless: Place current issues in a magazine rack or vertical desktop periodical boxes, and toss old ones into a pile for recycling. If you haven't read a certain article yet, tear it out rather than saving the entire issue.

FILE Clip articles you want to save and place them in an accordion file with subject labels such as Gardening, Travel, Finances, etc., plus one file labeled "To Read" for stories of general or pressing interest.

the little pieces

ORGANIZE Use a pouch with pockets or an accordion file for receipts for credit-card purchases, for items that you may want to return, and for tax purposes. You can also use these dividers to keep track of ATM slips; simply toss them after you balance your checkbook each month.

KEEP Use a binder with clear plastic sleeves to store product information: instruction manuals, warranties, and receipts. Staple each receipt to its respective warranty or manual so it doesn't get lost; you'll need it if the product has to be returned.

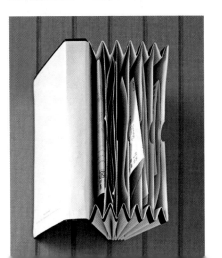

organization

Whether you're storing your paper clips or your personal contacts, there's a proper place for everything.

receptacles, boxes, and other kits

MULTIPLE COMPARTMENTS For clutter-phobes, a smart organizing system is one that includes subdivisions. On the desktop or in a desk drawer, make use of organizers with compartments of varying size and shape, so you're not shoving the scissors in too small a space or constantly searching for a paper clip.

SINGLE COMPARTMENTS If you prefer separate receptacles, such as a pencil cup for pens and pencils and a shallow box for Post-it notes, buy a low-sided tray that will accommodate all the elements within its borders.

addresses and calendars

WHO AND WHERE A Rolodex-style address "book" is ideal for desktop use. You can refer to telephone numbers and addresses at the flip of a card and easily keep the cards updated. Use a pencil to create new entries, so you can erase them as people and businesses move on, or staple business cards directly to the entry cards. Keep a pared-down list of important contacts in a portable address book or PDA for when you're on the go.

WHEN Planners, designed to sit on your desktop or hang on your wall or bulletin board, will help you keep track of a week's (or month's) worth of appointments at a time and avoid double-booking.

simple solutions

MAGNETIC ATTRACTION
Glue a metal ruler to your bulletin board and affix a magnetized storage bin to it. You'll save yourself some valuable desktop real estate.

SHELVES AND BOXES
Shelves and vertical periodical boxes conserve desk space. Organize catalogs and periodicals by category for quick reference.

CD/DVD STORAGE
If you like to have CDs and DVDs on hand while you work but don't like them in piles, organize them in a tray that fits neatly in a file drawer.

KEYPAD ORGANIZER
If desk-drawer storage is at a premium (or nonexistent), buy a keypad organizer that includes a hidden compartmentalized tray. (Make sure the product is compatible with your computer before purchasing.)

ALL-PURPOSE STATIONERY KIT
Fill an attractive box with note cards and paper, envelopes, a pen (or pens), stamps, and a self-inking return-address stamp or preprinted adhesive address labels. Place the box on top of the desk or within a desk drawer.

FILE BOX
A fabric-covered file box that accommodates both letter- and legal-size folders makes work look more like play, and even sits pretty on a shelf.

the laundry room

It's the spot in your house where so much becomes clean—whites get brighter, linens get crisper, and stains disappear. Needless to say, the best, most effective laundry room is itself tidy and well organized.

(It's hard *not* to feel like a scullery maid when toiling in the basement under a flickering fluorescent light, wielding a gooey bottle of detergent.) With a few easy systems and devices, plus a small stash of multi-tasking products, even a cluttered corner for dirty clothes will be transformed into a streamlined, clean, attractive laundry room. So attractive, in fact, that it might even entice some other family member into tackling a couple of loads.

MELANIE ACEVEDO page 77

ANTONIS ACHILLEOS page 57, bottom middle; page 141

JAMES BAIGRIE page 13; page 20; page 23, top middle; page 41, top middle; page 41, bottom right; page 51, top; page 52, top; page 52, middle; page 55, top; page 55, middle; page 56; page 62; page 65; page 68, top; page 68, bottom; page 71, middle; page 72, bottom; page 79; page 81; page 82, top middle; page 82, bottom middle; page 83, top middle; page 83, top right; page 83, bottom left; page 83, bottom middle; page 83, bottom right; page 91; page 93, top middle; page 93, top right; page 93, bottom right; page 103; page 105, middle; page 105, bottom; page 106; page 107; page 115, top; page 118, top left; page 118, bottom left; page 118, bottom right; page 119, bottom left; page 119, bottom middle; page 119, bottom right; page 130; page 137, bottom middle; page 148, middle

ROLAND BELLO page 136

MONICA BUCK page 37, bottom; page 123

ANITA CALERO page 39

SUSIE CUSHNER page 87; page 94; page 100; page 118, top middle

DANA GALLAGHER page 28; page 32; page 40; page 57, top middle

TRIA GIOVAN: page 154, top right

THAYER ALLYSON GOWDY page 74; page 82; page 88; page 149

BOB HIEMSTRA page 4; page 19; page 24; page 26; page 41, bottom left; page 109; page 111; page 115, middle; page 116, top; page 117; page 118, bottom middle; page 119, top left; page 119, top middle; page 119, top right; page 146; page 147, top; page 147, middle; page 147, bottom

FRANCES JANISCH page 36; page 37, top; page 37, middle; page 52, bottom; page 53; page 61; page 66; page 71, top; page 73; page 84; page 104

THIBAULT JEANSON page 105, top

SARAH MAINGOT page 38, bottom

CHARLES MARAIA page 51, bottom; page 82, bottom right; page 154, bottom left

SCOGIN MAYO page 113; page 114; page 115, bottom; page 116, middle; page 116, bottom

JOSHUA MCHUGH: page 49; page 57, top left

JEFF MCNAMARA page 35; page 41, top left; page 57, bottom right; page 118, top right; page 142; page 148, top; page 154, top middle; page 154, bottom right

MINH & WASS page 93, bottom middle

AMY NEUNSINGER page 128, middle; page 129

DAVID PRINCE page 10; page 16, top; page 16, middle; page 16, bottom; page 17; page 22; page 23, bottom left; page 23, bottom middle; page 23, bottom right; page 41, bottom middle; page 72, top; page 72, middle; page 82, bottom left; page 83, top left; page 148, bottom; page 150; page 151, top; page 151, bottom; page 152, top; page 152, middle; page 152, bottom; page 153; page 154, top left

MARIA ROBELDO page 127; page 128, top; page 133; page 137, top left

FRANCE RUFFENACH page 23, top left; page 93, top left; page 137, top right; page 137, top middle; page 137, bottom right; page 154, bottom middle

ELLEN SILVERMAN page 41, top right; page 58; page 67; page 98

MIKKEL VANG page 6; page 46; page 57, bottom left; page 124; page 137, bottom left

WILLIAM WALDRON page 31; page 50; page 90; page 120; page 128, bottom

WENDELL T. WEBBER page 57, top right; page 68, middle; page 80; page 82, top left

PAUL WHICHELOE page 9; page 14; page 23, top right; page 38, top; page 38, middle; page 42; page 45; page 51, middle; page 54; page 55, bottom; page 70; page 71, bottom; page 92; page 93, bottom left; page 97; page 135; page 138; page 145; page 151, middle; page 155

clothing-care
essentials

STAIN REMOVER

Even the most fastid-
ious among us will
eventually spill ketchup
on her shirt. Keep
stain removers on your
laundry-room shelf:
a solvent (such as
Shout) for greasy
stains and an enzyme
treatment (such as
Biz) that eats away at
protein stains.

WHITENING AGENT

Use chlorine bleach
with discretion: It
may make your clothes
look whiter, but it
can also harm them by
slowly eating away
at fibers and actually
yellowing—rather
than brightening—
them over time. Try a
color-safe nonchlorine
bleach or enzyme
treatment instead.

DETERGENT

For the bulk of your
laundry, an old
standby detergent,
such as Tide or Wisk,
will keep colors bright
as well as specialty
detergents do. To best
activate the detergent,
wash in warm or hot
water; detergents
don't work as well in
water below sixty-five
degrees.

MILD SOAP

A mild soap, such
as Woolite or baby
shampoo, is required
for delicate knits
and lingerie, which
should be hand-
washed and dried
on a flat surface.
Never throw these
garments in the wash-
ing machine, even
on the delicate cycle.

DISTILLED WATER

Whether you're on a
well or a municipal
system, impurities in
tap water can stain
your clothes when
you iron or steam with
it, so distilled water
is preferable. (It
also won't clog the
inside of your iron or
steamer.) A scented
distilled water can
add a subtle fragrance
to your clothes.

SPRAY STARCH

When it comes time
to iron, a spray starch
not only keeps your
cottons and linens
looking crisp but also
creates a smoother
surface for the iron to
do its work.

LINT ROLLER

A lint roller made of
sectioned adhesive
tape is ideal for most
clothes. Because tape
can sometimes leave
a residue, use a lint
brush on finer fabrics.

DEPILLER

A battery-operated
or electric depiller
will quickly remove
pilled fibers from
your delicate knits
without damaging
them. Shave in a
circular motion on a
hard surface.

basics

helpful additions

HAMPERS AND SORTERS

Each bedroom clothes closet in your home should have a light-weight hamper or canvas bag that can be carried to the laundry room and emptied there. You will also want a large central hamper, permanently stationed in your laundry room, to hold accumulated clothing. Buy a three-bin sorter, and ask family members to separate their dirty clothing into categories (whites, colors and darks, and delicates). Hampers and sorters should be made of a breathable fabric, such as canvas, and have soft edges that won't nick walls or shins or snag clothing.

SHELF

A long shelf or set of shelves should be reachable with little effort. If you must place supplies on a shelf high above the washer and dryer, consider a collapsible step stool for easy access. Arrange items on the shelf from left to right in order of use: stain remover, then detergent and bleach or other whitening agent, fabric softener (if you use it), spray starch or sizing, and distilled water. Never keep bleach near ammonia (which you shouldn't use with laundry anyway). Their combined fumes can be toxic.

TUB

A basin or sink in the laundry room provides convenient access to water, but it's not the best choice for hand-washing and presoaking. A small, shallow heavy-duty plastic tub—one that fits within your sink for easy filling— conserves water and prevents your sink (although not your drainpipe) from being exposed to the chemicals in cleaning agents and solvents.

DRYING RACKS

Collapsible drying racks, made for air-drying delicate items, are easy to fold up and store after use. Wooden racks have a nice look but wear easily; opt for a rust-free metal model that can withstand the weight of washed clothing and be moved outdoors for fresh-air drying. In small laundry rooms, place clothing on a tabletop drying mesh (which can be collapsed for storage) on a utility table.

IRON AND IRONING BOARD

Many ironing boards look alike, but you want to find the right one for your needs. Some have an attached cradle for a hot iron to rest in, but the cradle will most likely get in your way while you iron. A tabletop mini–ironing board is an exercise in frustration: It's too small to accommodate adult-size clothing and doesn't withstand pressure well. Your iron should have a nonstick coating that will help it glide smoothly across clothing, steam and mist functions to soften wrinkles, a sturdy cord that won't pull out of the socket easily, and an auto-matic shutoff control in the event that the iron is accidentally left unattended.

To dry in a dryer or on a clothesline? To rest on a hanger or a hook? Whatever your washing and drying needs, there's a laundry-room tool to do the trick.

baskets, bins, and boxes

LABEL Small items, such as sewing kits and lint rollers, can be put in labeled baskets on shelves to keep them from getting dusty or misplaced. Bins and boxes are similarly helpful in this regard.

STORE Drawers are only moderately useful in a room that holds so many bottles and boxes, although under-sink storage is a good place to stow products used to clean the laundry room itself.

hangers, clothespins, hooks

HANG Clothes that are air-dried on hangers (even after partial drying in the dryer) are less likely to shrink and will have fewer wrinkles to iron out later.

ATTACH Clothespins help you evenly clip items such as bulky bed linens to a clothesline; for delicates, use pins with fabric-edged clamps to avoid damaging the material. (To prevent wet clothes from bumping into each other, you can also put a garment on a hanger and use a clothespin to hold the hanger to the line.)

HOOK Clothing that needs to be steamed can be hung on a hook on a wall, which will keep the item from swinging and free both hands to do the job.

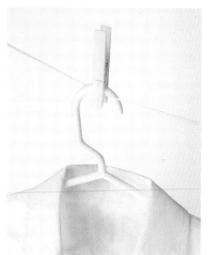

clothesline

CONCEAL A clothesline is ideal for clothes and bedding that require (or benefit from) full or partial air-drying. Get a retractable one that can be installed unobtrusively on a wall, or use an outdoor line and take advantage of the fresh air and sun.

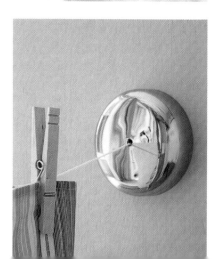

simple solutions

SAFETY PRECAUTIONS

Clothes will be less susceptible to damage if you take the time to button buttons, zip zippers, and empty pockets before laundering.

BLEACH PEN

Rather than splash bleach all over your stained white blouse, use a bleach pen with a tiny applicator tip to make a direct hit on the offending spot.

NAIL POLISH

Apply clear nail polish to the thread on both sides of a button to help reduce wear on the fibers and keep the button in place.

MESH BAGS

Keep track of each family member's clothes by washing and drying them in separate cotton-mesh bags.

SEPARATE LOAD

Wash towels separately to keep their lint off clothes. To maintain their shape, remove them from the dryer when they are still slightly damp.

TOWEL SETS

To save on energy and avoid over-laundering, assign one towel and one washcloth per person per week in your household. Each family member can have a set in a different color.

SHEET CONTROL

The number of sheet sets per bedroom should never exceed three: one on the bed, one in the hamper or in the process of being washed, and one in the linen closet, ready for use.

HAND WASH

Hand-washing silk and rayon is better for the fabric than dry-cleaning. After washing in cold water, lay the garment flat to dry. When the fabric is almost dry, use a warm iron on the reverse side.

TOWEL WRAP

Roll a hand-washed sweater in a towel, which will absorb excess moisture, then lay the sweater flat to dry completely.

CYCLES

When drying clothes in an older-model dryer, opt for the permanent-press or wrinkle-free cycle, which adds cooling air toward the end and helps keep clothes from wrinkling. (In new models, cool air follows most cycles.)

FOLDING TABLES

A deep, wide tabletop is essential for properly folding and stacking clothes. Avoid folding freshly laundered clothes on top of the washer and dryer, which are often magnets for unwanted dust and lint.

SEWING KIT/BASKET

Keep a sewing kit in the laundry room for quick fixes. As you inspect clothes for stains before they go in the wash, you will be more likely to notice holes, small tears, and loose buttons that can be corrected with needle and thread.

the storage room

THE STORAGE ROOM   Despite what it may have become, your storage room—attic, basement, or garage—was not actually built to be a catchall for everything that doesn't fit elsewhere in your house. These rooms have specific functions (including, of course, storage) and should be as well planned and maintained as the tiniest kitchen cupboard or bedroom closet. If you think of storage areas as vital support systems for the rest of your house, you'll see that they will serve you better if you equip them properly. As with the more visible—and likely more beautiful—rooms in a home, a storage room that's clean and well organized is one that will serve you best.

METAL SHELVING
Easy to assemble and affordable, metal shelving units withstand heat and humidity better than wood while keeping your valuables safe from pipe leaks or basement flooding. Look for lightweight but sturdy chrome units (a favorite in hectic restaurant kitchens).

PLASTIC STORAGE BOXES
Cardboard boxes, no matter how strong, bend and dent with frequent use and eventually succumb to dampness. Waterproof plastic containers protect their contents better, seal tighter, and are easy to carry and move around on shelves (as long as they aren't too big). Choose ones with snap-on lids and built-in handles. Clear plastic allows you to see what's inside; otherwise, label containers with self-adhesive stickers.

SAFETY-PROTECTION DEVICES
It's prudent to install smoke detectors and fire extinguishers in your storage room, where heat, water, electrical wires and cords, and combustible materials are often in close proximity. You should also consider carbon-monoxide alarms, particularly near gas-powered appliances, such as a water heater or a washer and dryer.

PORTABLE LAMP
A portable lamp equipped with a long, often retractable cord, a hook, and a protective metal or rubber sheath can be your best friend in a storage room. If an attic lightbulb goes out or if you simply need to retrieve something from an especially dark corner, you can light the way yourself. The lamp can then be hung by its hook, freeing your hands to work on other things.

DEHUMIDIFIER
Basements and garages are particularly susceptible to humidity and moisture. A self-draining humidifier keeps things dry and helps fight mildew and odors.

five easy pieces

organization

If your storage room is packed to the ceiling, you probably won't be able to make it tidy in a single afternoon. Don't let this space overwhelm you—simply take it on a little bit at a time.

decluttering 101

STEP 1 Start by creating three categories: Donate, Keep, and Toss. Go through each item in the space and assign it to one of the three. If you rarely use a piece, it's probably a good candidate for the Donate or Toss category.

STEP 2 Call up local charities and arrange for a pickup of items in the Donate category; put the Toss items out with the trash or recycling.

STEP 3 Edit the Keep pile down further into new categories, such as Sporting Equipment, Power Tools, Tax Returns, etc.

STEP 4 Assess how you will store these items. Sporting equipment, for example, might go in a wall cabinet or a bin in a corner of the garage; power tools might be hung on a system of hooks on a large piece of pegboard in the basement; tax returns might be assigned to a plastic storage box placed on a high shelf or in a corner of the attic.

STEP 5 Assign specific areas in the storage room to house these items.

STEP 6 Label whatever is not plainly identifiable. It is all too easy to forget where you put something, such as a box of Christmas ornaments, if you don't need to access it frequently.

hooks and pegs

HANG In addition to a comprehensive arrangement of shelves and storage containers, hooks and pegs are an ingenious, inexpensive way to create order out of disorder in the attic, basement, and garage. Consider suspending the following from the ceiling, shelves, or the back of a door: bicycles, cords, hoses, tools, strollers, shovels, work gloves, fire extinguishers, fishing rods, rolls of wrapping paper, and bolts of fabric.

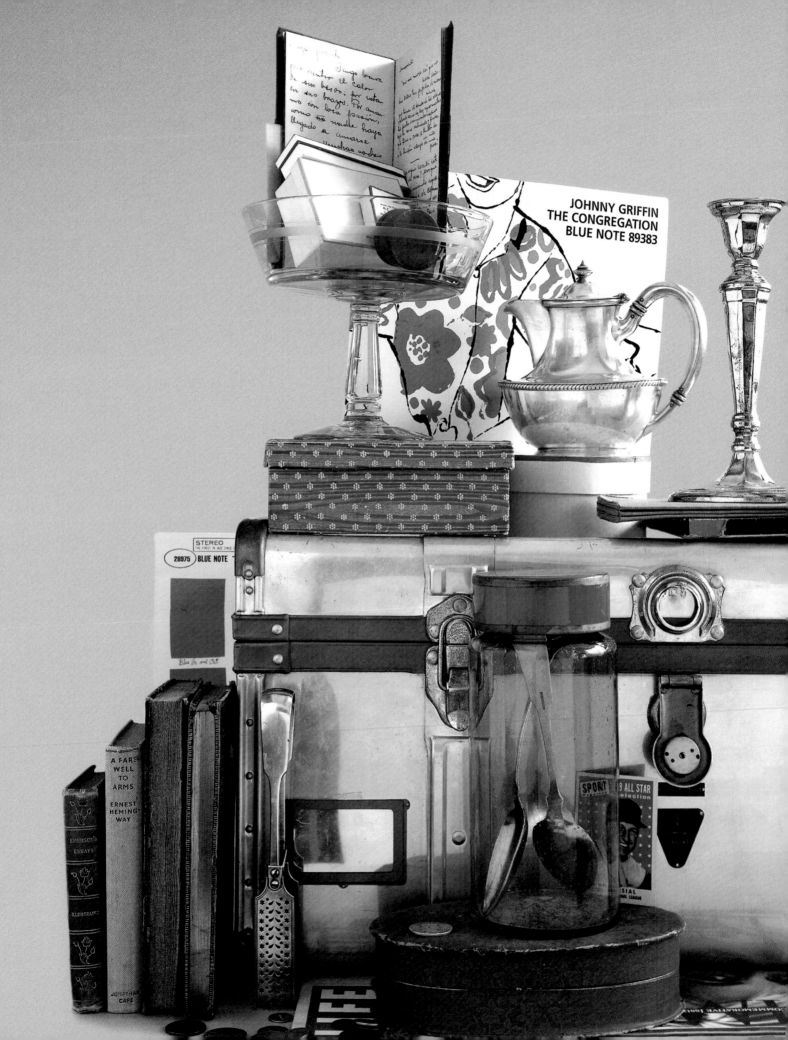

JOHNNY GRIFFIN
THE CONGREGATION
BLUE NOTE 89383

STEREO
THE FINEST IN JAZZ SINCE
28975 BLUE NOTE

Blue Up and Out

A FAREWELL TO ARMS
ERNEST HEMINGWAY

EMERSON'S ESSAYS

ILLUSTRATED

JONATHAN CAPE

SPORT
ALL STAR
Selection

TWO-PRONGED HOOK

Hang bulky items, such as a vacuum cleaner, on a sturdy two-pronged hook that is designed to accommodate uneven weights.

METAL BRACKET

Create a storage corner by affixing a metal bracket to the wall and stowing both short- and long-handled tools either on it or behind it.

TARP

Chances are you won't be able to fit your antique rocking chair into a storage container, no matter how hard you try. A plastic tarp can be your savior: It will protect a large, unwieldy item from dirt, debris, and even some moisture. Place the piece on a wooden pallet or cinder blocks to keep the bottom out of harm's way.

FLASHLIGHT

A flashlight can be indispensable in a storage room, particularly if your power goes out and you need to reach a fuse box, or if you need to illuminate a dark corner.

TOTE

Repurpose a little-used tote bag by storing cloths and rags used for cleaning inside it.

SNAP-LOCK STRIP

Install a bracket with snap-lock grips on a storage room door. It will keep long-handled tools, such as brooms and mops, firmly in place.

streamlining systems

recycling

There are few things that provide maximum satisfaction with minimal effort the way recycling can. Even so, the sorting, stacking, stashing, and hauling can sometimes make recycling feel like a backbreaking endeavor. But it's worth the effort. The number of landfills in the United States has dropped by about 62 percent since 1988, and now nearly one-third of the nation's solid waste is recycled. Set up a proper recycling system and the effort will always be worth it.

preparation...

1. DO YOUR HOMEWORK.
Check with your local collection center to find out what it accepts and rejects. Be aware: Residents in some areas face fines for not recycling.

2. POST LOCAL GUIDELINES. They are a good reminder for your family, and the quick reference makes recycling easier. Use a Magic Marker to highlight what goes where.

3. STUDY YOUR TRASH.
What you use most will determine the container types and sizes you'll require. If you drink a lot of soda but don't read many newspapers, for example, you'll want a larger bin for cans and bottles than for paper.

4. CREATE CONVENIENCE.
Ideally, your home recycling center will be a two-part system: one for everyday disposal and the other for storage. (See Pick a Storage Space, below.) The everyday disposal center should be placed where you generate the most waste; for many, that's the kitchen. Containers should be as accessible as the trash can (ideally, right next to it). Sorting is a necessary evil of recycling, so why do it twice? Get a divided container that lets you separate as you dispose. If you are short on space, consider hanging sturdy, washable canvas bags on the inside of a pantry door.

5. PICK A STORAGE SPACE.
When your kitchen bins fill up, move their contents to a storage spot until it's time to drop them off at the curb or a center. Consider the garage, laundry room, mudroom, or utility closet. Your containers should be easy to transport, so look for ones with wheels. If your community has return deposits on cans and bottles, separate them, too, for returns.

as you shop...

1. SKIP SINGLE-SERVING ITEMS.
These require more packaging (and therefore unnecessary waste) per unit.

2. PURCHASE JUICE CONCENTRATES.
You supply the water and the pitcher—and skip the large plastic container.

3. AVOID DISPOSABLE GOODS.
These include razors, lighters, and plastic plates.

4. USE YOUR OWN CANVAS OR STRING BAGS FOR GROCERY SHOPPING.
If you do use plastic, return it to the store for recycling; most stores have collection spots. Paper bags can be used to hold other paper for recycling.

5. USE PRODUCE BAGS SPARINGLY.
Save them for moist or small, loose items, such as lettuce and berries.

6. CLOSE THE LOOP.
Purchase products that were themselves made from recycled materials. For example, Seventh Generation makes paper products from 100 percent recycled materials.

as you separate…

1. **RINSE.** Clean the container if it held food or drink.

2. **REDUCE VOLUME.** Break down boxes, crush cans, and flatten plastic bottles, unless your return-deposit laws mandate that cans and bottles must be intact.

3. **DON'T GO OVERBOARD.** Most recycling centers ask only that the main recyclables (plastic, paper, metal, and glass) be separated from one another, rather than sorted within each group.

PLASTICS

- Look at the bottom of most plastic containers and you'll find the triangular-arrows recycling logo around a number. Most programs will recycle numbers 1 and 2; numbers 3 to 7 are less likely to be recycled and should be reused or discarded.

PAPER

- Check with your local program to see which kinds of paper are accepted.
- If your center accepts mixed paper, you can include post-cards, greeting cards, and junk mail.
- Newspapers can be bundled or placed in brown paper bags for collection.
- Some phone-book distributors offer special services for recycling last year's book.
- Don't recycle paper products that have food on them (pizza boxes with stalactites of cheese on the lid, for example)—it contaminates the paper.

METALS

- Recycle aluminum (most beverage cans, pet-food cans, aluminum foil, take-out containers, and disposable baking pans) and steel bi-metal (beer and soft-drink cans).
- Some programs require that canned goods have their labels removed.
- Aerosol cans and paint cans must be completely empty.
- No magnetic metal is recyclable. You can test a metal simply by holding a magnet to it; if it sticks, don't recycle it.

GLASS

- Separate by color only if your local center requires it.
- Labels do not have to be removed.
- Steel and plastic lids must be removed but can usually be recycled with like materials.
- Most household glass, such as windows, ceramics, light-bulbs, mirrors, drinking glasses, and Pyrex, cannot be recycled.

donate, ditch, or sell?

What do you throw out, give away, or sell? Clothes you don't—or won't—wear anymore; books you didn't like enough to finish; and toys your kids no longer touch. You don't want any of this stuff, and you could almost certainly use the space it takes up. Remember: By getting rid of these and other items, you can make money, earn tax deductions, or help a worthy cause. And for what's truly useless, there are ways to throw out your things while doing as little damage to the environment as possible.

appliances

DONATE Goodwill Industries, the Salvation Army, and other charities accept small appliances (toasters, mixers) in working condition. Policies on accepting large appliances (washers, dryers) vary by location, so check with local branches.
TRASH Call your sanitation department or visit its website to find out about large-item pickup and local dump sites. Or go to www.recycle-steel.org to find a large-appliance recycler near you.

baby items

DONATE Items for infants and children—from diapers (clean) to strollers—are highly sought after by charity-run thrift shops.
SELL Clothes and accessories in excellent condition are also in demand at specialty consignment shops.

books

DONATE Books are accepted by Goodwill and the Salvation Army, not to mention schools, libraries, literacy programs, hospitals, and senior centers.
SELL Try your luck at local used-book stores (bear in mind that you'll rarely get what you paid), or, if you have rare or collectible titles, sell them on Amazon.com or eBay.

clothes

DONATE Nationwide, Goodwill, the Salvation Army, and Vietnam Veterans of America accept all kinds of clothing in good condition. Also check with churches, local hospitals, women's shelters, and agencies that work with the homeless to see if they have clothing-donation programs.
SELL If you have like-new designer clothes, a wedding dress, or a great collection of Levi's you want to unload, it might pay to sell the items on consignment. Consignment shops tend to be selective but, as a result, sell a large percentage of the merchandise they accept and get good prices for it.

cds and records

DONATE Both Goodwill and the Salvation Army accept donations of recorded music.
SELL Try used-CD shops or online vendors. Keep in mind that on eBay or Amazon, a run-of-the-mill CD rarely fetches more than $5. Factor in the site's charge to the seller and the hassle of mailing to the buyer and decide if it's worth your time. The CD Exchange (www.thecdexchange.com) offers an easier alternative: E-mail them a list of the CDs you want to sell (they should be in excellent condition, with liner notes), and the CD Exchange will respond within 24 hours, telling you up front what it will pay (in cash or merchandise credit). You mail the CD Exchange the discs, and it sends you a check.

computers

DONATE Check with your local Goodwill, Salvation Army, or Muscular Dystrophy Association (www.mdausa.org) for their donation guidelines. The National Cristina Foundation (www.cristina.org/dsf/) places refurbished computers in educational and nonprofit organizations for people with special needs.
SELL Computers are the fifth-best-selling category on eBay. If your hardware is really up to date, it could be worth the effort of putting it up for sale online.
TRASH If your computer is more than five years old, it's probably best to recycle. Organizations such as the Computer Recycling Center (www.crc.org) accept obsolete computers and recycle unusable parts to keep them out of landfills. Visit www.sharetechnology.org/information.html for a listing of refurbishers and recyclers.

eyeglasses

DONATE Lions Clubs International (www.lions clubs.org) has collection boxes at various community offices and businesses, Goodwill Industries stores, and LensCrafters stores (www.lenscrafters.com). Check with local chapters for more information.

furniture

DONATE Goodwill and the Salvation Army accept furniture in good condition (not broken, torn, stained, or faded). Although these are national organizations, furniture-donation standards and pickup policies vary by region, so check with local branches. Group homes and shelters may also accept donations.

TRASH To dispose of furniture in bad shape, call your sanitation department or visit its website to find out about large-item pickup and dump sites. Or check the Yellow Pages (try "Surplus and Salvage Merchandise") to find someone to haul it away.

kitchen equipment and household goods

DONATE Goodwill and the Salvation Army are excellent resources for donating most household items.

SELL Certain high-end brands can fetch a decent price online. If you want to get rid of like-new All-Clad stainless-steel pans, for example, it might be worthwhile to offer them on eBay. Or look for a used-cookware dealer in your area.

musical instruments

DONATE Check with local branches of the Muscular Dystrophy Association and local schools. Other organizations to try: The Directory of Youth Orchestras (http://metroyouth symphony.org/others.shtml); Mr. Holland's Opus Foundation (www.mhopus.org); and Music in Schools

Today/MUST (www.mustcreate.org).

SELL See what comparable items are selling for on auction sites to decide if this is the way to go.

sporting goods and exercise equipment

DONATE Organizations that accept sporting equipment and gear include Goodwill, the Salvation Army, youth programs, school athletic programs, disabled-athlete organizations, camps for sick children, Boys and Girls Clubs, and Scout Troops.

SELL If you have top-notch equipment in good condition, try selling online or through your local newspaper.

toys and games

DONATE Goodwill and the Salvation Army are glad to accept toys in good shape and games that have all their pieces.

SELL Consignment shops that specialize in children's merchandise will often take toys in good condition. While eBay has a busy toy marketplace, prices for noncollectibles tend to be on the low side. Consider the time, effort, and cost involved.

tips to start decluttering

Clutter is that stuff you don't notice, use, or care about until it's time to get rid of it. Yet at that precise moment, although you know better, letting go of your *Riverdance* instructional video or those 25 blank notepads feels like smothering a piece of your soul. You are plagued with concerns: What if you need it someday? Why did you buy it? What would *Antiques Roadshow* say? Enough is enough. Clutter clouds your mind, trips you up, slows you down, and devours the stuff surrounding it. Carting the junk away is the easy part. Overcoming the mental block is what's hard. Use these strategies to get you going.

1. act like you're moving

Say you had to uproot and relocate. What would you take with you? You don't actually have to pack anything up—just set aside the few things that you love and use and see what's left over. Try this with your cookbooks, for example: Pull out the ones that are tenderly tattered due to years of use, then look at the ones still on the shelf. Ask yourself if you would pay someone to haul away those you've been keeping because they were gifts or because you felt ambitious when you bought them. If not, sell them to a used-book store or donate them.

TOSS-IT TIPS

▪ Envision your home as a prospective buyer might: Uncluttered spaces make the best first impression. They're also a lot easier to keep clean and dust-free.

▪ Imagine the potential buyer (or worse, a relative) going through your closets or drawers. What would you not want him or her to see?

▪ Buy containers and baskets only after you've decided what to keep. This way you'll have a much better sense of the kind of storage you need.

WHY IT WORKS

▪ You don't have to get rid of things you love or need — you just have to determine what those things are.

▪ If you've ever packed and paid for a move, the motivation for paring down your possessions will be all too clear.

2. assess your rooms

Walk through your house with a pen and a notebook, writing down the activities that take place in each room and the items associated with those activities. Remove anything that doesn't relate to your proposed activity for that space. If you want to use your bedroom only for sleeping and getting dressed, relocate anything that doesn't relate to that: documents stored in the closet, a trade journal you've been meaning to read, sewing supplies, or anything else that distracts you from the main purpose of the room.

TOSS-IT TIPS

▪ Start with one room, but keep the whole house in mind.

▪ Think of rooms that have multiple purposes as several smaller areas, so it's clear where items should be returned if they stray. If gift-wrapping is the designated activity for a certain part of the study and you find a spool of ribbon in the kitchen, you'll know exactly where it belongs, and so will other family members.

WHY IT WORKS

▪ This strategy lays the foundation for long-term change.

▪ Tackling clutter without knowing your priorities can be counterproductive. It is important to understand the difference between organizing and rearranging.

3. clean out for a worthy cause

Getting rid of things will be easier if you can picture someone else benefitting from them (instead of how they just signify wasted money for you). Pick an organization to donate to and learn as much as you can about it. Read the literature, check out the website, or visit the facility.

TOSS-IT TIPS

▪ Don't just leave your stuff outside the charity's storefront or in a donation bin. Deliver it in person, or find out if the organization will arrange a pickup from your home.

- See if there are specific items the charity needs; this will make those things easier to give up. If it doesn't accept certain items—such as that combination NordicTrack/clothes hanger—ask if it knows of a group that does.
- If an item is truly worthless or beyond repair, don't make the organization deal with it. Find out the proper way to junk it instead.
- Get your kids involved, too, so they can see what it's like to give.

WHY IT WORKS
- The items you discard will most likely be used, worn, or appreciated a lot sooner in someone else's hands than they would in yours.
- You can earn a tax deduction for donated goods. But you are responsible for keeping track of donations, determining their worth, and itemizing them on your tax return.

4. make organizing a team event

Find a friend or two who support your organizational goals and who have decluttering needs of their own, and take turns organizing each other's homes: Your house this weekend, your friend's the next. If you can't find a willing friend, consider teaming up with a professional organizer—it could be money well spent.

TOSS-IT TIPS
- Make sure everyone is compatible and knows the difference between encouragement and coercion.
- The owner of the item in question should have the final say on whether it gets tossed.

WHY IT WORKS
- Your friends don't have the same sentimental attachment to your stuff that you do.

- It's fun having someone to listen to the story of why you're so emotionally attached to, say, a chipped Pyrex nesting bowl—before you put it in the giveaway pile.

5. go shopping in your closet

If you have a lot of clothes that you never wear but you keep finding yourself in yet another T.J. Maxx dressing room, try shopping at home instead. Next time you're putting away laundry or dry cleaning, grab an armful of clothes that you haven't worn since you can't remember when and try them on in front of a full-length mirror. Put the ones that you would want to buy again back into circulation; donate the rest.

TOSS-IT TIPS
- Don't keep anything that is permanently stained, ill-fitting, or beyond repair.
- Don't let the mere fact that you paid a lot guilt you into keeping something. Your closet is prime real estate.

WHY IT WORKS
- You have to deal with only a few items of clothing at a time—not your whole closet.
- If your weight has fluctuated over the years, this method lets you pinpoint what fits now and bag memories of your body-size history.
- You might enjoy it, especially if you unearth a long-buried treasure.

the shelf-life periodic table

The expiration dates in this chart are offered as a rough guideline. The shelf lives of most products depend on how you treat them. Edibles, unless otherwise indicated, should be stored in a cool, dry place. (With any food, of course, use common sense.) Household cleaners also do best in a dry place with a stable temperature. After the dates shown, beauty and cleaning products are probably still safe but may be less effective.

Pb — Peanut butter, natural
U/O: 9 months.

Jf — Peanut butter, processed (Jif)
U: 2 years.
O: 6 months; refrigerate after 3 months.

Hny — Honey
U/O: Indefinite shelf life.

Bsg — Brown sugar
U/O: 4 months

Wr — Worcestershire sauce
U: 5 to 10 years.*
O: 2 years.

Kof — Coffee, instant
U: Up to 2 years.
O: 2 weeks.

Cof — Coffee, canned ground
U: 2 years.
O: 2 months refrigerated.

Caf — Coffee, gourmet
Beans: 3 weeks in paper bag, longer in vacuum-seal bag.*
Ground: 1 week in sealed container.

Mu — Mustard
U/O: 2 years.*

Oil — Olive oil
U: 6 months.
O: 4 to 6 months.

Tb — Tabasco
U/O: 5 years, stored in a cool, dry place.

Sld — Salad dressing, bottled
U: 12 months after "best by" date.
O: 3 months refrigerated.

Ch — Chocolate (Hershey bar)
U/O: 1 year from production date.

T — Tea bags (Lipton)
U/O: Use within 18 months of opening the package.

Mml — Marshmallows
U/O: 3 months.

Wdx — Windex
U/O: 2 years.

Kp — Ketchup
U: 1 year.*
O: 4 to 6 months.*

Vgr — Vinegar
U: 2 years.
O: 1 year.

Tu — Tuna, canned
U: 1 year from purchase date.
O: 3 to 4 days, not stored in can.

Ma — Maraschino cherries
U: 3 to 4 years.
O: 2 weeks at room temperature; 6 months refrigerated.

Stk — Steak sauce
U/O: 6 to 12 months.*

Sd — Soda, regular
U: In cans or glass bottles, 9 months from "best by" date.
O: Doesn't spoil, but fizz is affected.

Pwr — Protein bars (PowerBars)
U: 10 to 12 months. Check "best by" date on the package.

Wp — Wood polish (Pledge)
U/O: 2 years.

Myo — Mayonnaise
U: Indefinitely.
O: 2 to 3 months from "purchase by" date.*

Soy — Soy sauce, bottled
U: 2 years.
O: 3 months.*

J — Juice, bottled (apple or cranberry)
U: 8 months from production date.
O: 7 to 10 days.

Olv — Olives, jarred (green with pimento)
U: 3 years.
O: 1 to 2 months.

Fd — Frozen dinners
U: 12 to 18 months; best if used in 3 to 4 months.

Dsd — Diet soda (and soft drinks in plastic bottles)
U: 3 months from "best by" date.
O: See Sd, above.

Ps — Dried pasta
U/O: 2 years.

Mr — Mr. Clean
U/O: 2 years.

Pkl — Pickles
U: 1 year.
O: No conclusive data. Discard if slippery or excessively soft.

Wn — Wine (red, white)
U: 3 years from vintage date; 20 to 100 years for fine wines.
O: 1 week refrigerated and corked.

Br — Beer
U: 4 months.

Pn — Peanuts
U: 1 to 2 years unless frozen or refrigerated.
O: 1 to 2 weeks in airtight container.

Fv — Frozen vegetables
U: 8 months.
O: 1 month.

Mpl — Maple syrup, real or imitation
U/O: 1 year.

Ri — Rice, white
U/O: 2 years from date on box or date of purchase.

Mp — Metal polish (silver, copper, brass)
U/O: At least 3 years.

*After this time, color or flavor may be affected, but the product is still generally safe to consume.

Wnd — Wash 'n Dri moist wipes
U: 2 years.
O: Good until dried out.

Legend:
- food
- household product
- beauty product
- U unopened
- O opened or used
- U/O unopened or opened

Pa — Paint
U: Up to 10 years.
O: 2 to 5 years.

Np — Nail polish
U/O: 1 year.†

Fn — Foundation, oil-based
U/O: 12 months.†
Water-based
U/O: 18 months.†

Bdl — Body lotion
U/O: 3 years.

Bg — Bath gel, body wash
U/O: 3 years.†

Mw — Mouthwash
U/O: Three years from manufacture date.†

Bl — Bleach
U/O: 3 to 6 months.

Ld — Liquid dish detergent
U/O: 1 year.

Spr — Spray paint
U/O: 2 to 3 years.

Npr — Nail-polish remover
U/O: Lasts indefinitely.

Ls — Lipstick
U/O: 2 years.

Sh — Shampoo
U/O: 2 to 3 years.

Ba — Bath oil
U/O: 1 year.

Ws — Tooth-whitening strips
U/O: 13 months.

Ll — Liquid laundry detergent
U: 9 months to 1 year.
O: 6 months.

Pl — Powdered laundry detergent
U: 9 months to 1 year.
O: At least 6 months.

Mtr — Motor oil
U: 2 to 5 years.
O: 3 months.

Pfm — Perfume
U/O: 1 to 2 years.

Lb — Lip balm
U: 5 years.
O: 1 to 5 years.

C — Conditioner
U/O: 2 to 3 years.

Bsp — Bar soap
U/O: 18 months to 3 years.

Shv — Shaving cream
U/O: 2 years or more.

Pd — Powdered dish detergent
U/O: 1 year.

Mg — Miracle Gro, liquid
O: 3 to 8 years.
Water-soluble
U/O: Indefinite.

Ant — Antifreeze, premixed
U/O: 1 to 5 years.
Concentrate
U/O: Indefinite.

Msc — Mascara
U: 2 years.
O: 3 to 4 months.

Eyc — Eye cream
U: 3 years.
O: 1 year.

Hs — Hair spray
U/O: 2 to 3 years.

D — Deodorant
U: 2 years.
O: 1 to 2 years.
For antiperspirants, see expiration date.

Ra — Rubbing alcohol
U/O: At least 3 years.

Aer — Air freshener, aerosol
U/O: 2 years.

Bt — Batteries, alkaline
7 years.
Lithium
10 years.

Fx — Fire extinguisher, rechargeable
Service or replace every 6 years.
Nonrechargeable
12 years.

Bb — Body bleaches and depilatories
U: 2 years.
O: 6 months.

Fl — Face lotion
U/O: With SPF, see expiration date. All others, at least 3 years.

Hg — Hair gel
U/O: 2 to 3 years.

† For beauty products, all dates are from the manufacture date, which is either displayed on the packaging or can be obtained by calling the manufacturer's customer-service number.

31-41
42-57
68-85
90-93
105-106
105

CLOSETS
108-119

shopping guide

Think of this guide as the introduction to a world of ease, order, and calm. Many of these stores are located in major cities across the country, so check your local listings. Most also have terrific websites for shopping or browsing. Listings for national stores have the general information number; the local store number is listed for those with just one location. Whether you are organizing, decorating, or just looking for a few helpful additions, these resources are sure to provide some solutions.

ABC CARPET AND HOME
212-473-3000
www.abchome.com
Home furnishings, bath and linens, carpet cleaning, custom draperies and upholstery, gifts and accessories

ANTHROPOLOGIE
800-309-2500
www.anthropologie.com
Home furnishings, gifts and accessories

BANANA REPUBLIC
888-277-8953
www.bananarepublic.com
Home furnishings, kitchen and dining, gifts and accessories

BARNES AND WAGNER
866-253-6560
www.barnesand
wagner.com
Gifts and accessories

BED, BATH & BEYOND
800-462-3966
www.bedbathand
beyond.com
Home furnishings, bath and linens, kitchen and dining, gifts and accessories

BENJAMIN MOORE PAINTS
800-826-2623
www.benjaminmoore.com
Paints, flooring

BLACK & DECKER
800-544-6986
www.blackanddecker.com
Appliances, cleaning and supplies

BLOOMINGDALES
800-232-1854
www.bloomingdales.com
Home furnishings, kitchen and dining, bath and linens, gifts and accessories

BODUM INC.
800-232-6386
www.bodum.com
Kitchen and dining, gifts and accessories

BOMBAY COMPANY
800-829-7789
www.bombaycompany.com
Home furnishings, bath and linens, gifts and accessories

BREWSTER WALLCOVERING COMPANY
800-366-1700
www.brewsterwall
covering.com
Wall coverings

BROADWAY PANHANDLER
866-266-5927
www.broadwaypan
handler.com
Kitchen and dining, gifts and accessories

CALIFORNIA CLOSETS
888-336-9709
www.california
closets.com
Closet customization service and accessories

CALVIN KLEIN HOME
800-294-7978
Home furnishings, baths and linens, gifts and accessories

CHAMBERS
800-334-9790
www.williamssonomainc.
com/com/chm/index.cfm
Home furnishings, bath and linens, gifts and accessories

CHARLES P. ROGERS
800-582-6229
www.charlesprogers.com
Home furnishings, linens, gifts and accessories

CITE DESIGN
212-431-7272
www.cite-design.com
Home furnishings, kitchen and dining, gifts and accessories

CLOSET FACTORY
310-715-1000
www.closetfactory.com
Closet customization service and accessories

CLOSETMAID
800-874-0008
www.closetmaid.com
Closet customization service and accessories

THE COMPANY STORE
800-289-8508
www.thecompany
store.com
Home furnishings, bath and linens, gifts and accessories

THE CONTAINER STORE
888-266-8246
www.containerstore.com
Home furnishings, bath and linens, kitchen and dining, gifts and accessories (storage and organization)

COST PLUS WORLD MARKET
800-267-8758
www.costplus.com
Home furnishings, kitchen and dining, bath and linens, gifts and accessories

COUNTRY FLOORS
800-311-9995
www.countryfloors.com
Flooring

COUNTRY SWEDISH
888-807-9333
www.countryswedish.com
Home furnishings, wall coverings, gifts and accessories

CRATE & BARREL
800-996-9960
www.crateandbarrel.com
Home furnishings, kitchen and dining, bath and linens, gifts and accessories

CUDDLEDOWN OF MAINE
800-323-6793
www.cuddledown.com
Home furnishings, bath and linens, gifts and accessories

DESIGN WITHIN REACH
800-944-2233
www.dwr.com
Home furnishings, bath and linens, kitchen and dining, floor coverings, gifts and accessories

DWELL
www.dwellshop.com
Home furnishings, bath and linens

EXPOSURES
800-572-5750
www.exposuresonline.com
Photo supplies, gifts and accessories

FILOFAX
877-234-2426
www.filofaxusa.com
Organizers, stationery, gifts and accessories

FORTUNOFF
800-367-8866
www.fortunoff.com
Home furnishings, bath and linens, kitchen and dining, gifts and accessories

GARNET HILL
800-622-6216
www.garnethill.com
Home furnishings, bath and linens, gifts and accessories

GLOBAL TABLE
212-431-5839
www.globaltable.com
Tabletop and home accessories

GRACIOUS HOME
800-338-7809
Home furnishings, kitchen and dining, bath and linens, cleaning and supplies, appliances

HOLD EVERYTHING
800-421-2285
www.holdeverything.com
Home furnishings, bath and linens, kitchen and dining, gifts and accessories (storage and organization)

THE HOME DEPOT
800-553-3199
www.homedepot.com
Home furnishings, cleaning and supplies, floor coverings, appliances, kitchen and dining, bath and linens, installation services, design services, contractor services, tool rental

IKEA
800-434-4532
www.ikea.com
Home furnishings, kitchen and dining, bath and linens, floor coverings, gifts and accessories

JONATHAN ADLER
877-287-1910
www.jonathanadler.com
Home furnishings, kitchen and dining, floor coverings, gifts and accessories

KATE'S PAPERIE
888-941-9169
www.katespaperie.com
Stationery, gifts and accessories

KMART
866-562-7848
www.kmart.com
Home furnishings, cleaning and supplies, kitchen and dining, bath and linens, appliances, gifts and accessories

LAND'S END
800-356-4444
www.landsend.com
Home furnishings, kitchen and dining, bath and linens, gifts and accessories

LINENS-N-THINGS
866-568-7378
www.lnt.com
Home furnishings, bath and linens, kitchen and dining, appliances, gifts and accessories

L.L. BEAN
800-809-7057
www.llbean.com
Home furnishings, bath and linens, kitchen and dining, gifts and accessories

MACY'S
800-622-9748
www.macys.com
Home furnishings, kitchen and dining, bath and linens, appliances, gifts and accessories

shopping guide

MTS FRAMES
800-242-7173
www.mtsframes.com
Photo supplies and framing, gifts and accessories

NEIMAN MARCUS
800-685-6695
www.neimanmarcus.com
Home furnishings, kitchen and dining, bath and linens, gifts and accessories

NICOLE FARHI
212-223-8811
www.nicolefarhi.com
Home furnishings, gifts and accessories

PEARL RIVER
800-878-2446
www.pearlriver.com
Kitchen and dining, gifts and accessories

PIER 1 IMPORTS
800-245-4595
www.pier1.com
Home furnishings, kitchen and dining, bath and linens, gifts and accessories

PINE CONE HILL
413-496-9700
www.pineconehill.com
Home furnishings, kitchen and dining, bath and linens, gifts and accessories

POTTERY BARN
888-779-5176
www.potterybarn.com
Home furnishings, kitchen and dining, bath and linens, gifts and accessories

PURE DESIGN
780-483-5644
www.puredesign
online.com
Home furnishings, gifts and accessories

RALPH LAUREN HOME
888-475-7674
www.polo.com
Home furnishings, bath and linens, gifts and accessories

RESTORATION HARDWARE
800-762-1005
www.restoration
hardware.com
Home furnishings, cleaning and supplies, bath and linens, floor coverings, gifts and accessories

ROOM & BOARD
877-465-0555
www.roomandboard.com
Home furnishings, baths and linens, gifts and accessories

RUBBERMAID
888-895-2110
www.rubbermaid.com
Home furnishings, bath and linens, kitchen and dining, cleaning supplies, gifts and accessories
(storage and organization)

SMITH & HAWKEN
800-776-5558
www.smithand
hawken.com
Home furnishings, gifts and accessories

SMITH & NOBLE
800-560-0027
www.smithandnoble.com
Home furnishings, bath and linens, floor coverings, gifts and accessories

STACKS & STACKS
800-761-5222
www.stacksandstacks.com
Home furnishings, kitchen and dining, bath and linens, appliances, gifts and accessories

TAKASHIMAYA NEW YORK
800-753-2038
Home furnishings, kitchen and dining, gifts and accessories

TARGET
800-800-8800
www.target.com
Home furnishings, cleaning and supplies, kitchen and dining, appliances, bath and linens, gifts and accessories

THE TERENCE CONRAN SHOP
866-755-9079
www.conran.com
Home furnishings, kitchen and dining, gifts and accessories

TUMI
800-322-8864
www.tumi.com
Gifts and accessories, luggage

UMBRA
800-387-5122
www.umbra.com
Home furnishings, kitchen and dining, bath and linens, gifts and accessories

WATERWORKS
800-998-2284
www.waterworks.com
Home furnishings, kitchen and dining, bath and linens, gifts and accessories

WEST ELM
866-937-8356
www.westelm.com
Home furnishings, kitchen and dining, bath and linens, gifts and accessories

WILLIAMS-SONOMA
877-812-6235
www.williams
sonoma.com
Home furnishings, kitchen and dining, bath and linens, appliances, cleaning and supplies, gifts and accessories

photography credits

MELANIE ACEVEDO page 77

ANTONIS ACHILLEOS page 57, bottom middle; page 141

JAMES BAIGRIE page 13; page 20; page 23, top middle; page 41, top middle; page 41, bottom right; page 51, top; page 52, top; page 52, middle; page 55, top; page 55, middle; page 56; page 62; page 65; page 68, top; page 68, bottom; page 71, middle; page 72, bottom; page 79; page 81; page 82, top middle; page 82, bottom middle; page 83, top middle; page 83, top right; page 83, bottom left; page 83, bottom middle; page 83, bottom right; page 91; page 93, top middle; page 93, top right; page 93, bottom right; page 103; page 105, middle; page 105, bottom; page 106; page 107; page 115, top; page 118, top left; page 118, bottom left; page 118, bottom right; page 119, bottom left; page 119, bottom middle; page 119, bottom right; page 130; page 137, bottom middle; page 148, middle; page 160; page 165; page 166, top left; page 166, top right; page 166, bottom right; page 167, top left; page 167, bottom left; page 167, bottom middle; page 167, bottom right; page 177, bottom left

ROLAND BELLO page 136

MONICA BUCK page 37, bottom; page 123

ANITA CALERO page 39; page 175

SUSIE CUSHNER page 87; page 94; page 100; page 118, top middle

DANA GALLAGHER page 28; page 32; page 40; page 57, top middle

MICHELE GASTL page 159; page 164; page 167, top middle

TRIA GIOVAN: page 154, top right

THAYER ALLYSON GOWDY page 74; page 82; page 88; page 149

BOB HIEMSTRA page 4; page 19; page 24; page 26; page 41, bottom left; page 109; page 111; page 115, middle; page 116, top; page 117; page 118, bottom middle; page 119, top left; page 119, top middle; page 119, top right; page 146; page 147, top; page 147, middle; page 147, bottom

FRANCES JANISCH page 36; page 37, top; page 37, middle; page 52, bottom; page 53; page 61; page 66; page 71, top; page 73; page 84; page 104

THIBAULT JEANSON page 105, top

RICK LEW page 178

MARK LUND page 177, top right

SARAH MAINGOT page 38, bottom

CHARLES MARAIA page 51, bottom; page 82, bottom right; page 154, bottom left

PETER MARGONELLI page 168; page 171; page 173

SCOGIN MAYO page 113; page 114; page 115, bottom; page 116, middle; page 116, bottom

JOSHUA MCHUGH: page 49; page 57, top left

PATRICK MCHUGH page 163; page 167, top right

JEFF MCNAMARA page 35; page 41, top left; page 57, bottom right; page 118, top right; page 142; page 148, top; page 154, top middle; page 154, bottom right

MINH & WASS page 93, bottom middle

AMY NEUNSINGER page 128, middle; page 129

DAVID PRINCE page 10; page 16, top; page 16, middle; page 16, bottom; page 17; page 22; page 23, bottom left; page 23, bottom middle; page 23, bottom right; page 41, bottom middle; page 72, top; page 72, middle; page 82, bottom left; page 83, top left; page 148, bottom; page 150; page 151, top; page 151, bottom; page 152, top; page 152, middle; page 152, bottom; page 153; page 154, top left; page 166, top middle; page 174, bottom; page 176; page 177, top left; page 177, bottom middle; page 177, bottom right

MARIA ROBELDO page 127; page 128, top; page 133; page 137, top left

FRANCE RUFFENACH page 23, top left; page 93, top left; page 137, top right; page 137, top middle; page 137, bottom right; page 154, bottom middle

ELLEN SILVERMAN page 41, top right; page 58; page 67; page 98; page 166, bottom left

TARA STRIANO page 174, top; page 174, middle

MIKKEL VANG page 6; page 46; page 57, bottom left; page 124; page 137, bottom left

WILLIAM WALDRON page 31; page 50; page 90; page 120; page 128, bottom; page 156

JONELLE WEAVER page 177, top middle

WENDELL T. WEBBER page 57, top right; page 68, middle; page 80; page 82, top left; page 166, bottom middle

PAUL WHICHELOE page 9; page 14; page 23, top right; page 38, top; page 38, middle; page 42; page 45; page 51, middle; page 54; page 55, bottom; page 70; page 71, bottom; page 92; page 93, bottom left; page 97; page 135; page 138; page 145; page 151, middle; page 155

REAL SIMPLE

MANAGING EDITOR Kristin van Ogtrop
CREATIVE DIRECTOR Vanessa Holden
SPECIAL PROJECTS EDITOR Sarah Humphreys
DESIGN DIRECTOR, SPECIAL PROJECTS Eva Spring
COPY EDITOR Myles McDonnell
RESEARCH EDITOR Westry Green

PUBLISHER Steven Sachs
ASSOCIATE PUBLISHER, ADVERTISING Kevin White
GENERAL MANAGER Tina Pace
CONSUMER MARKETING DIRECTOR Kristiana Helmick
VICE PRESIDENT, PR AND COMMUNICATIONS
Kristen Jones Connell
PRODUCTION DIRECTOR Tracy Kelliher

TIME INC. HOME ENTERTAINMENT

PUBLISHER Richard Fraiman
EXECUTIVE DIRECTOR, MARKETING SERVICES Carol Pittard
DIRECTOR, RETAIL & SPECIAL SALES Tom Mifsud
MARKETING DIRECTOR, BRANDED BUSINESSES Swati Rao
DIRECTOR, NEW PRODUCT DEVELOPMENT Peter Harper
FINANCIAL DIRECTOR Steven Sandonato
ASSISTANT GENERAL COUNSEL Dasha Smith Dwin
PREPRESS MANAGER Emily Rabin
BOOK PRODUCTION MANAGER Suzanne Janso
PRODUCT MANAGER Victoria Alfonso
ASSOCIATE PREPRESS MANAGER Anne-Michelle Gallero

This book was produced by Melcher Media, Inc.
124 West 13th Street, New York, NY 10011
www.melcher.com
PUBLISHER Charles Melcher
EDITOR IN CHIEF Duncan Bock
PROJECT EDITOR Lia Ronnen
PUBLISHING MANAGER Bonnie Eldon
EDITORIAL ASSISTANT Lauren Nathan
MARKET EDITOR Olga Naiman

ART DIRECTION AND DESIGN Vanessa Holden and Eva Spring
COVER DESIGN mgmt.
COVER STYLING Elizabeth Mayhew
ILLUSTRATIONS Alicia Cheng and Jason Lee

SPECIAL THANKS Bozena Bannett, Ron Broadhurst, David Brown,
Glenn Buonocore, June Cuffner, Michael Hargreaves, Jean Herr,
Andrea Hirsh, Elizabeth Johnson, Robert Marasco, Brooke McGuire,
John Meils, Jacklyn Monk, Claudio Muller, Jonathan Polsky,
Chivaughn Raines, Ilene Schreider, Lindsey Stanberry, Shoshana
Thaler, Adriana Tierno, Britney Williams, Megan Worman.

SPECIAL THANKS TO THE FOLLOWING STORES
The Container Store, Crate & Barrel, Garnet Hill, Jonathan
Adler, and Waterworks

Copyright © 2006 by Time Inc. Home Entertainment
Cover photography copyright © 2004 Anita Calero
Photography © 2004 by those specifically listed on page 191

Published by Real Simple Books, a trademark of Time Inc.
1271 Avenue of the Americas, New York, NY 10020

ISBN: 1-933405-36-8

We welcome your comments and suggestions about Real
Simple Books. Please write to us at:

> Real Simple Books
> Attention: Book Editors
> P.O. Box 11016
> Des Moines, IA 50336-1016

If you would like to order any of our hardcover Collector's
Edition books, please call us at 1-800-327-6388 (Monday
through Friday, 7:00 A.M.–8:00 P.M. or Saturday, 7:00 A.M.–6:00 P.M.
Central Time).